MARRIAGE IN THE LORD

A Catholic Formation Resource

Seventh Edition

Leisa Anslinger
Laura Boyce-Steinhauser
Sandra Dooley
Christopher J. Ferraro
Mary G. Fox
Kim Haggerty
Frank P. Hannigan
Steven D. Monaghan
Lauri Przybysz
Lorie Simmons
William Steinhauser
Dora Tobar
Kyle S. Turner

Nihil Obstat
Rev. Mr. Daniel G. Welter, JD
Chancellor
Archdiocese of Chicago
April 22, 2020

Imprimatur
Most Rev. Ronald A. Hicks
Vicar General
Archdiocese of Chicago
April 22, 2020

The *Nihil Obstat* and *Imprimatur* are declarations that the material is free from doctrinal or moral error, and thus is granted permission to publish in accordance with c. 827. No legal responsibility is assumed by the grant of this permission. No implication is contained herein that those who have granted the *Nihil Obstat* and *Imprimatur* agree with the content, opinions, or statements expressed.

Liturgy Training Publications is grateful for the assistance of the Archdiocese of Chicago's Office of Divine Worship and Office of Lifelong Formation and to Leisa Anslinger in the development of this resource; to Brian Wells and David Petro for their review of and input to the financial section; and to Mary G. Fox for her review of and input to the communication section.

MARRIAGE IN THE LORD: A CATHOLIC FORMATION RESOURCE, SEVENTH EDITION © 2020 Archdiocese of Chicago: Liturgy Training Publications, 3949 South Racine Avenue, Chicago, IL 60609; 800-933-1800; fax: 800-933-7094; email: orders@ltp.org; website: www.LTP.org. All rights reserved.

This book was edited by Danielle A. Noe. Michael A. Dodd was the production editor, and Juan Alberto Castillo was the designer and production artist. Music engraved by Michael Ruzicki.

Cover art by Tracy Walker; chapter headings and footers by Martin Erspamer, OSB; icons by Juan Alberto Castillo; interior art on pages 16, 39, 40 and 42 by Bandelin-Dacey Studios; page 44 by Jim Burrows; pages 6, 12, 25, 28, 31, 43, 44, 45, 48, 55, 60, 69, and 71 by Martin Erspamer, OSB; page 47 by James B. Janknegt; page 33 by Andrew Lewis © Liturgy Training Publications; page 67 by Sheena Magnesen; page 68 by Anna Manhart © Liturgy Training Publications; pages 8 and 22 by Cody F. Miller; page 66 by Rush Photos; page 50 by Boris Stoilov, pages 3, 17, 42, 43, and 45 by Kathy Ann Sullivan; page 54 by Paula Wiggins.

24 23 22 21 20 1 2 3 4 5

Printed in the United States of America

Library of Congress Control Number: 2020934599

ISBN: 978-1-61671-576-2

MTL

Contents

Preparing to Be Married

You are engaged to be married! What a wonderful blessing. Congratulations! In this time of preparation, you are sure to have many things on your mind and in your heart, most especially the love you have for each other. It is good to be reminded that the love that unites you as a couple is a gift from God. When you experience overflowing, overwhelming love for your fiancé, you have a glimpse of the boundless love God has for you and for all of humanity.

Aside from your commitment to grow in faith in Jesus Christ and live a Christian life, making a commitment to one another in marriage is the most important decision you will ever make. Let that sink in for a moment. While much of your attention and energy right now is focused on the wedding, the time you spend in prayer, reflection, conversation, and learning from others in the coming months will help you live a loving, fruitful life as a married couple. Like the decision to follow Jesus Christ, which requires ongoing commitment and leads to a stronger relationship that directs your life, so too in marriage you and your loved one will make daily decisions together—some momentous and others mundane. With each new step together, your relationship will deepen, and your love will grow stronger. This life is directed by your love for Christ, and it takes practice and requires a firm foundation. This is why marriage preparation is so important. Think of the sessions of this process as building blocks to establish this firm foundation for your marriage.

A Resource for Your Needs

This book has been written with you in mind! Throughout this book, you will be invited to reflect on the prayers and ritual moments that will be part of your wedding celebration.[1] Your wedding ceremony will take place in the presence of God and within the prayer of the Church. The prayers, music, scripture readings, and ritual moments reveal the meaning behind the important commitment you are ready to make. Because the liturgical texts, symbols, and gestures shape our understanding of marriage, reflecting on these elements before your wedding will help you prepare more deeply for married life.

Sections of this book are devoted to helping you create a vision for your marriage; develop a greater appreciation of marriage as a sacrament; grow in the ways you communicate with each other, resolve conflicts, and manage money; consider the many dimensions of sexuality and intimacy in marriage; make or renew a commitment to live as disciples of our Lord together; and establish goals for a healthy and joy-filled marriage. Keep this book as a journal and a reminder of the many facets of marriage you will consider in this time of preparation. Return to these pages often, especially in the early years following your wedding, as you grow in love and experience the natural ups and downs of married life. You can revisit the content and the questions included in this book throughout your marriage to reflect upon and strengthen your commitment to one another and to God.

A Marriage that is desired, prepared for, celebrated, and lived daily in the light of faith . . . is . . . sealed by a blessing.

—*Order of Blessing an Engaged Couple*, 11

The Preparation Process

Depending on your diocese or local parish, as part of your marriage formation you may be asked to participate in a weekend retreat or a day of formation with other couples. Or you might meet with a sponsor couple from your parish for

1. The prayer texts and scripture passages quoted throughout this resource are from the official Catholic ritual for marriage, *The Order of Celebrating Matrimony*. The numbers refer to the paragraph numbers in the ritual text.

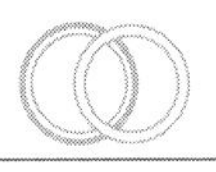

multiple one-on-one meetings. You will need to meet with your priest and parish music director (or director of worship or marriage coordinator) to prepare your wedding liturgy. You will probably be asked to take a class on Natural Family Planning (NFP).

Marriage preparation is not a class or a "one and done" experience. It is spiritual formation. The things you will experience during this time of preparation are steps toward a lifelong journey together. All that you share together during preparation will help form you as a couple. You will learn from the experience of other couples, consider many topics that will influence the way you approach marriage, and do all of this over time, with the grace of God and the presence of the Holy Spirit.

Some things may come up during this time of preparation that surprise you. You may find topics that are easy for you to talk about together and other issues that are more challenging. You might find areas of disagreement that you were unaware of and that need resolution. Whatever happens, promise yourself and each other that you will be honest and open, knowing that in doing so you are establishing patterns that will remain with you from this day forward. You will want to come back to this book again and again to help strengthen your commitment to one another.

Christ at the Center

This time of preparation will encourage you to put Christ at the center of your marriage. You might be people of deep faith; you may come to Mass occasionally but rarely think about God or talk with each other about faith; you may be participating in this marriage preparation process only to please your parents or grandparents, or because you want to be married in a church ceremony. No matter where you are on this spectrum of faith, this time of preparation is a good moment to open your heart to the Lord. Truly, every moment is a good time to do so! Especially now, as you are laying the foundation for the years of married life to come, it is good to make room for God. Imagine having a friend who walks with the two of you, sharing in your days and nights, holding you up when you feel lost, strengthening you in the challenging times of life, filling your heart with love. Jesus wants to be that friend, and so much more. Building your marriage with Christ at the center means that you are never alone, your life will be filled with grace and purpose, your marriage be rooted in love more than you can dream is possible.

The Church Is Here for You

At the beginning of the marriage liturgy, everyone who gathers for your wedding is invited to support and pray for you. As you picture yourself at your wedding, surrounded by family and friends, know that others stand with you as well. These people, some whom you will meet during preparation, including the marriage preparation team, mentor couples, and a priest or deacon, have made a commitment to help you lay a strong foundation for your married life. You may not yet know others within the faith community who will pray for you and those who help to provide support and formation for you and others throughout the many stages of life and faith. As Church, members of Christ's Body, we stand with one another in faith, love, and support, coming to rely on each other at every step on the journey, knowing that in doing so, we fulfill Christ's command to love one another as he loves us. Never hesitate to reach out when you need help or support in your marriage and the circumstances of life. Know that the Church is here for you, ready to share your joy, prepared to be with you in times of trial and grief, grateful that you are one with us in faith.

Your Family of Origin

There is a mystery about each of us. We are brought into being with the spark of our Creator—a beloved child of God, endowed with gifts, talents, and the desire to love and be loved. In God's wisdom, we are human, endowed with and susceptible to human strengths and weaknesses, human clarity and confusion. Especially as children, we are sensitive and impressionable—formed and framed by the circumstances and people with whom we grow up. Like a dry sponge in water, we have soaked up the behaviors and attitudes of the people who have surrounded us.

Now the mystery of you—brought into the world by God with your belovedness and endless possibilities, tempered and shaped by the family in which you grew up—now you seek to join yourself to the mystery of another person—also created by God with belovedness and endless possibilities, also tempered and shaped by a family. While you were growing up, you may never have noticed how you were being formed. But now on the threshold of forming a new family, you are invited to reflect on the mystery of who you are and how you came to be this particular person eager to love and be loved.

> **Members of Christ's faithful have special need of [God's] grace when they are preparing to form a new family.**
>
> —*Order of Blessing An Engaged Couple*, 224

The desires, expectations, attitudes, and habits you bring about with communication, arguing, money, sex, child raising, relations with extended family, and more come from your family of origin and will play a role in the way you will live your new married life. All of these matters make up part of your individual selves that each of you will both delight in and struggle to honor. "I will "love you" and "honor you / all the days of my life."[1] you will soon promise, which means you will respect and value each other—including everything you bring. Reflecting on where your expectations and attitudes come from and how you will work with them will give you a foundation for all the relationship work you will do in the future. And for this holy work, may you receive grace.

1. *The Order of Celebrating Matrimony*, 62.

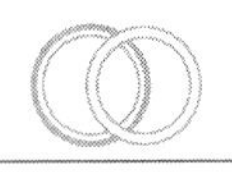

Couple's Discussion

It is important for your future spouse to have a sense of what your family life was like growing up. These experiences and shared values will influence your marriage. In a private, quiet, and safe environment, take some time to think about your answers to these questions and then discuss together.

1. Use three words or phrases to describe yourself.
2. Use three words or phrases others might use to describe you.
3. Would you describe yourself as more extraverted or introverted? Do you thrive around people? Or do you need a quiet space for internal reflection?
4. What three things do you appreciate about yourself?
5. What three things would you change about yourself?
6. Discuss the most significant event of your life.
7. Think about a person who has made a difference in your life. How is this person significant?
8. My family consists of (name them and think of immediate family and extended family).
9. Describe the proximity of your family (do they live nearby, are they scattered across the country or world, or in another area?).
10. Was religion important in your family? Did you pray together? Regularly attend Church services together?
11. Think about your relationship with your family members. Is your family close? Are there issues in your family? Are your family members flexible or inflexible?
12. Did you come from a stable family? Was there discord? divorce? separation?
13. Were you around children often? Did you babysit? Or were you an only child?
14. Disagreements and arguments are normal in every family. How did your family argue? (Did they yell? Did they compromise? Did a particular family member always give in?)
15. How do the members of your family handle stressful situations?
16. Has your family ever experienced a significant loss (death, fire, home, money issues)? How was it dealt with?
17. In your family, was money hard to come by?
18. Who took responsibility for providing for your family and parenting? Was it shared?
19. How were you disciplined as a child? Are you planning to integrate these methods into your future family life?

Continues on next page ▶

20. Was there any physical or mental abuse in your family? alcohol or drug abuse?
21. Describe the condition of your home growing up and the place where you live now (messy, tidy, spotless, cozily cluttered, etc.).
22. Do you prefer warm, temperate, or cold temperatures?
23. How did your family celebrate birthdays and holidays (think especially about the traditions surrounding Thanksgiving and Christmas)?
24. Are politics a common topic of conversation among family members? Are there polarized or common views among members?
25. What traditions were important to your family?
26. Is your immediate or extended family active (or very present) in your life?
27. What do you like about your family life that you would like to bring into your marriage?
28. What part of your family life do you not want to bring with you into your marriage?
29. Was religion an important part of your family life?
30. Did your family have animals? Why yes or not?
31. Did culture play a role in your family life? How?
32. Have you ever been in a significant relationship? Were you in love before? Have you ever been engaged? married? Why did the relationship end? What did you learn about yourself from this relationship? How did it impact your life?
33. Is there a story you would like to share with your future spouse so that he or she has a better sense of your own family life and how you grew up?
34. Based upon your own experiences, what are your expectations for married life?

    Think about these topics:

    - Going to Mass and praying together or as a family
    - Careers before and after children
    - Time to spend together
    - Financial responsibilities
    - Responsibilities for cleaning, laundry, and household repairs
    - Number of children
    - Animals
    - Location (buying a home, renting, relocating)
    - Family traditions, celebrating the holidays
    - Relationship with in-laws

Love is patient, love is kind.
It is not jealous, is not pompous,
it is not inflated, it is not rude,
it does not seek its own interests,
it is not quick-tempered, it does not brood over injury,
it does not rejoice over wrongdoing
but rejoices with the truth.
It bears all things, believes all things,
hopes all things, endures all things.
Love never fails.

1 Corinthians 13:4–8

SESSION 1
The Meaning of Christian Marriage

Liturgical Connection

Picture yourselves at your wedding ceremony. You have just exchanged your consent to marry (given your vows), and then the priest or deacon receives your consent and says:

> May the God of Abraham, the God of
> Isaac, the God of Jacob,
> the God who joined together our first
> parents in paradise,
> strengthen and bless in Christ
> the consent you have declared before
> the Church,
> so that what God joins together, no one
> may put asunder.[1]

This brief text says much about what we believe happens when a woman and man are united in marriage. God, who is love and who created you in love and for love, has brought you together. On your wedding day you will declare that you will commit yourselves to live in love for the rest of your lives. This love is more than a feeling of happiness or contentment, although love certainly often includes these emotions. The sort of love to which you are committing yourselves is love that is deep and lasting, far beyond the feelings of attraction, and takes you into the realm of the sacred. On the day of your wedding, as you hear this prayer, you will know that God will be with you throughout your life together.

Marriage as Sacrament

The sacraments of the Catholic Church are the primary ways we encounter God's grace, become one with Christ, and strengthen our relationship with God and each other. Participating in the sacraments, especially the weekly (or daily) celebration of the Eucharist, helps us be more like Christ. There are seven sacraments in the Church, and many of them are celebrated at significant moments in the life of the individual. For example, baptism celebrates our new life in Christ and the fact that we are children of God. Confirmation is a celebration of the coming and presence of the Holy Spirit in our lives, and reconciliation heals our broken relationship with God.

One of the many reasons you have been asked to participate in marriage preparation is that as Catholics, we understand marriage to be a sacrament for two baptized people. It is important to appreciate the sacramental nature of marriage and what this means for you in your life together. A sacrament is a sign of and sharing in the grace of God. In the celebration of sacraments, ordinary substances such as water, wine, bread, oil, the human voice, and touch are used to impart God's grace in indelible and lasting ways. Sacraments enable us to encounter Christ's presence and strengthen our relationship with God and with one another. In a very special way, you will encounter Christ and be united to one another in marriage. The union between you is to be a sign of God's union with the world.

In the sacrament of marriage, you consent to enter into union with one another through Christ. As in all sacraments, God's enduring love is made known and shared. In marriage, through your commitment and witness to love, you make God's loving presence known to one another, your families, and all with whom you interact. While all Christians are called to share Christ's love in the way they live their lives, marriage calls you to do so in a unique way, as a couple who willingly and freely are joined together. As you grow in love

1. *The Order of Celebrating Matrimony*, 64.

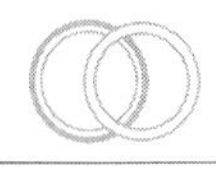

for one another, caring even when it is difficult to do so, sharing yourselves in service, giving of self and resources to those who are in need, living as Christ's people at home, work, and in the world, you communicate God's grace. This is a sacred call and carries with it responsibility and privilege.

Covenant

Understanding marriage as sacrament helps us grasp the difference between a Christian marriage and other marriages. When you commit yourselves to one another in the sacrament of marriage, you are united through and with the grace of God, living and active in your life.

Look back to the prayer at the beginning of this chapter. It speaks of the God of Abraham, Isaac, and Jacob. God made a covenant with Abraham and his descendants, declaring that his love is eternal. It does not die. You can walk away from God, but God will not walk away from you. Similarly, in marriage you enter into a covenant with one another. This is much deeper than a contract, in which each party agrees to certain things. In your covenant with one another, you promise that your love will endure through all of the joyful, happy moments as well as the sorrowful and challenging ones. In this covenant love, you promise that you will not walk away from each other, that you will love one another as God loves you. There is more to this than a simple statement of love. Entering into a covenant with one another unites you in a profound way, in which two become one, one body, one flesh.

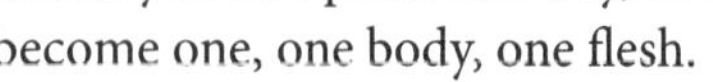

Self-Emptying Love

With all this talk of love, you might be thinking that love is all we need or love conquers all. Yet we know that love can be, and is supposed to be, demanding. Even a brief reading of the Gospels shows us that the sort of love Christ calls us to is not always easy. Jesus shows us that God's way of love requires us to love others as we love ourselves, to give freely of ourselves for the sake of the other. In marriage, we promise to embrace this way of love together.

Let us get really practical about this for a moment. Imagine yourself at the end of a long day. You're tired and stressed and cannot wait to go home and relax. Then, just as you enter the door of your home, your spouse calls from another room. He or she has been injured and needs to be taken to urgent care. Putting aside your need to rest, you take your loved one to the hospital, drive home past the pharmacy to pick up a prescription, and sit bedside until your spouse has fallen peacefully asleep. It is easy to imagine this sort of situation because you know it happens all the time. What is also easy to understand is that you can approach such a situation with a grumbling and selfish interior spirit—you are tired and don't have the patience to bear the situation gracefully—or with a willing and generous spirit, knowing that your spouse would do the same for you.

Jesus gave himself completely for our sake, accepting death on the cross in order to fulfill his mission of living God's love in the world. As Christian people, particularly as Christian spouses, you are called to empty yourself of selfishness, self-centeredness, and anything else that will prevent you from giving yourself freely and fully to your spouse and your family.

Paschal Mystery of Christ

Think of all you know about Jesus from the Gospels, your experience at Mass, and what you have been taught by your family and others. Jesus, the second person of the Holy Trinity, came to be one with us, to show and draw us into God's love so that we might live as God desires. Jesus taught people through words and actions—he healed the sick, forgave people's sins, showed God's mercy, and led people to put God at the center of their lives. Some saw that Jesus was the long-awaited Messiah and followed him. Some, however, met Jesus' compassion and mercy with derision, eventually plotting to have him killed. Jesus faced death on the cross with determination to fulfill his mission on earth, was crucified, died, and incredibly, rose on the third day. We call Christ's passion, death, and resurrection the Paschal Mystery. This is not a mystery as in something hidden that needs to be solved, but rather a mystery in that God's love is far beyond our understanding.

What does the Paschal Mystery have to do with your life together in marriage? Truly, you might say that it has everything to do with this! Because as you are joined to Christ through baptism, you also are called to hold firm to Christ's mission of compassionate love in the world. You are called to sacrifice, for each other, for your family, and for those in need. And as you answer the daily call to die to self for the sake of the other, you know that Christ is with you. As you experience the small deaths of not having everything as you would like, and the greater deaths of illness, failure, loss or lack of meaningful employment, and deaths of loved ones, you are assured that Christ is with you and that in time you will also experience the joy of new life, of resurrection.

The mystery of God's love for us in Christ is at the heart of who we are as members of Christ's Body, the Church. In baptism, we are united with Christ's mission of sacrificial love, sharing the compassion and mercy of the Lord through selfless service. When you enter into marriage, you are joined to one another in a similarly deep and lasting way. So much so that your union with each other is a reflection of Christ's union with the Church.

Vocation and Mission

Often, when we speak of vocation, we think first of the vocation of the priesthood or the call to consecrated religious life. Marriage, too, is a vocation, a way of responding to Christ's call to live in love. Vocation is always tied to mission—as you respond to Christ's call to enter into marriage, you also commit yourself to enter deeply into the love of God that unites you. This way of love is truly sacramental—you will encounter Christ's love in the relationship you share with one another and within your family, and through the witness of your love, you will communicate Christ's love to the world. You will explore this call to Christian love in marriage in the last chapter of this book.

By the Sacrament of Matrimony Christian spouses signify and participate in the mystery of unity and fruitful love between Christ and the Church.

—*The Order of Celebrating Matrimony*, 8

✦ VALIDITY OF THE SACRAMENT

In order for marriage to be a sacrament, it must take place between two baptized Christians who have come by their own free will, without impediments (such as a previous marriage), to marry in the Church. The couple must freely consent to marry with the intention of a lifelong commitment as well as being open to life. The marriage must be validly celebrated (that is, the wedding follows the Catholic ritual), and a priest or deacon and two additional witnesses (the witnesses are usually the maid [or matron] of honor and the best man) must witness the couple's exchange of consent to marry. Although a marriage between a Catholic and a person who is not baptized may be validly celebrated, it is not sacramental. In order for a sacramental marriage to take place, both parties must be baptized.

Couple's Conversation

1. ***Love is patient, love is kind.*** Be honest. Have you ever tried each other's patience? Are you sometimes less than kind to one another? Such moments will naturally happen in relationships. What helps you to pause, see the situation through the eyes of the other, and move toward patience and kindness?
2. ***Love is not jealous, is not pompous, it is not inflated, it is not rude, it does not seek its own interests.*** In marriage, you are called to seek the best for each other, to lift one another up, and lead each other toward God's way of peace, consolation, love, and mercy. How do you recognize and celebrate the gifts of one another? How do you complement each other so that each of you has opportunities to use your gifts in your relationship and in service of others? What situation comes to mind in which you focused on the accomplishments of the other, even when you were tempted to think only of yourself?
3. ***Love is not quick-tempered, it does not brood over injury.*** Everyone gets angry once in a while. In marriage, it is especially important to learn how to express and resolve anger between you. Your marriage will become stronger as you learn to communicate and work through conflict. When have you been angry with one another in the past? How did you resolve the situation? Do you quietly brood within yourself about unresolved experiences of anger between you or with others? How might you help each other let go of such feelings of anger, resentment, or conflict?
4. ***Love does not rejoice over wrongdoing but rejoices in the truth***. It is easy to fall into routines that are not healthy or holy individually or within your marriage. Things like alcohol or substance abuse, giving preference to work or other friends, or withdrawing from each other rather than addressing conflict or differing opinions can derail your marriage. How do you challenge each other when you feel the other is falling into negative behavior or patterns? What commitment do you make to each other to grow toward health and holiness?
5. ***Love bears all things, believes all things, hopes all things, endures all things.*** You may have already experienced trial, grief, illness, or challenge together. You are sure to do so in the future. What situation or circumstance has shown you the depth of your love and support for each other thus far?
6. ***Love never fails.*** It might seem easy to tell each other that love will conquer every difficulty and dark moment in life. As you prepare to enter into marriage, think about the difference the love you have for each other makes in your day-to-day life, through the natural ups and downs, and in the more momentous occasions as well. In what ways is the love you share a reflection of Christ's self-giving, enduring love?
7. Unfailing love is not static, nor is it easy to describe or to adequately convey in words. In this time of preparation for the sacrament of marriage, what commitment do you make to one another to live and grow deeply in love, now and throughout your life together?[2]

---

2. Questions are based on 1 Corinthians 13, an option for the second reading at your wedding liturgy.

Session 2

The Gift of Intimacy and Its Responsibilities

 Liturgical Connection

During your wedding liturgy, you will receive the Church's blessing on the physical expression of your love. This blessing, called the nuptial blessing, will take place after the praying of the Lord's Prayer. The priest or deacon will come before you and raise his hands over you in a gesture of blessing. The blessing calls for the Holy Spirit to come down upon you and strengthen you in the holiness that comes from marriage, and the Church prays that you will enjoy and cherish one another and are strengthened by friendship, mutual respect, and equal partnership.

May these your servants
hold fast to the faith and
keep your
commandments;
made one in the flesh,
may they be blameless in
all they do;
and with the strength
that comes from
the Gospel,
may they bear true witness
to Christ before all.

—*The Order of Celebrating Matrimony*, 74 (Nuptial Blessing)

Your sexual desire for each other and your marital embrace are God's gifts to you. May you make love a reality in your home and in your children. Children born into such a loving and peaceful home will be a blessing to society.

 Sexual Intimacy

Throughout the ages, Catholic teaching has been positive about the goodness and beauty of lovemaking. Conjugal love is the ultimate form of communication between a man and woman who have made a public, lifelong commitment. In their marriage bed, the couple turn to each other with a trusting vulnerability that says, "Here I am." In their lovemaking, the spouses consummate what they said at the altar, in the words of the exchange of consent (what many refer to as the "vows"), "I . . . take you." Always bear in mind that the other is not a possession but a precious gift.[1]

The wedding liturgy calls the union of the couple "the one blessing not forfeited by original sin or washed away by the flood."[2] In expressing their love sexually, the spouses are "speaking" with their bodies by giving the gift of themselves to one another. The concept that sexual union is part of the "language" of the body is part of St. John Paul II's teaching about marriage, referred to as the "Theology of the Body." He said, "The body, in fact, and it alone is capable of making visible what is invisible, the spiritual and divine. It was created to transfer in the visible reality of the world, the invisible mystery hidden in God from time immemorial, and thus to be a sign of it."[3]

Sexual intimacy in marriage takes time and practice. Fortunately, the spouses have made a vow to keep learning and growing as lovers for the rest of their lives. We can say that a married couple will live the sacramental quality of their marriage by becoming ever better lovers. Practice tenderness and appreciation. Maintain the displays

1. *The Order of Celebrating Matrimony*, 62.
2. *The Order of Celebrating Matrimony*, 74.
3. Pope John Paul II, "General Audience," Wednesday, February 20, 1980, Vatican City. Available from w2.vatican.va/content/john-paul-ii/en/audiences/1980/documents/hf_jp-ii_aud_19800220.html.

of affection that you showed when dating. Show affection and thoughtfulness. Keep your friendship alive.

Cultivate intimacy that lasts throughout the day. Develop a close relationship beyond sexual intercourse. Be willing to try new ways of expressing your love for each other. In every marriage, there will be times when sexual union is not possible or even desired by one or both partners. The dimensions of your spousal relationship are spiritual and emotional as well as physical. Whether or not you make love every day, your mutual giving should be a daily event. The daily victory against self-centeredness is another step toward oneness in mind, body, soul, and spirit. Pope Francis counsels engaged couples:

> Matrimony is [a] work of everyday; I could say a craftwork, a goldsmith's work, because the husband has the task to make his wife more woman, and the wife has the task to make her husband more man. To grow also in humanity, as man and as woman. And this is done between you. It is called growing together. This doesn't come from the air! The Lord blesses it, but it comes from your hands, from your attitudes, from your way of living, from your way of loving one another. Make yourselves grow! Always act so that the other grows.[4]

Respect your spouse. When people marry, they retain their human freedom. The Church calls husbands and wives into a partnership of equal dignity. They are both created in the image and likeness of God (see Genesis, chapters 1 and 2). While many spouses understand this call to mutuality and equal authority in marriage, others enter marriage with destructive attitudes about how men and women should relate to one another. Know that violence is never allowed, and forcing is contrary to the goal of lovemaking.

Sexual relations between spouses is a good and beautiful gift from our Creator. The positive message about sex has not always been well communicated. Some misunderstood biblical passages, such as "Wives should be subordinate to their husbands" (Ephesians 5: 22), seem to be a call for domination and submission. A fuller understanding of the relationship that God hopes for your marriage includes the previous verse, "Be subordinate to their husbands as to the Lord" (Ephesians 5:21). St. Paul expected that married couples would treat each other with the same dignity as any brother or sister in the Lord, "Love one another with mutual affection; anticipate one another in showing honor" (Romans 12:10).

In embracing conjugal life and in accepting and educating their children, they help one another to become holy and have their own place and particular gift among the People of God.

—*The Order of Celebrating Matrimony*, 8

Nourish intimacy in your marriage by a sensuous sexual relationship. A satisfying sex life involves paying attention to the other person and growing in appreciation of him or her as a beautiful creation of God. Be sensitive to one another's total needs. This conjugal relationship is potentially a source of deep satisfaction and joy that stimulates both growth and unity in marriage.

4. Pope Francis, "Address to Engaged Couples Preparing for Marriage," St. Peter's Square, Friday, February 14, 2014,

Couple's Conversation

1. What physically attracts you to your partner? Everything ♡
2. How do you feel about your sexuality?
3. How do you feel about your partner's sexuality?
4. In what ways are you a warm, considerate, and loving person?
5. How has your background influenced your sexual attitudes?
6. How do you see male or female differences influencing your sexual relationship?
7. How can you communicate your sexual needs and feelings to one another?
8. How can you develop a more unselfish and giving attitude about your sexuality?
9. How can intercourse be an experience that brings you closer to God?
10. In what ways can your sexual relationship be (a) uplifting, (b) healing, (c) a communion, (d) spiritual, (e) sanctifying?
11. What is one step you make that will allow you to spend more quality time together for communication and sharing of your feelings about your sexual relationship?
12. How do you show affection toward your significant other?
13. Are you comfortable discussing your needs for intimacy and physical closeness?
14. Do you have any worries about sexual intimacy?
15. How will you keep the romance alive in your relationship?

Commitment and Cohabitation

We in the Catholic community are glad that you are getting married. The wedding liturgy is clear that your marriage is not only important to both of you, but also to all of us, too. At the beginning of the wedding liturgy, the priest (or deacon) will turn to you, your future spouse, the wedding party, and your guests, and declare that the Church is happy for you and that God is present in your union. He will then offer the collect (or opening prayer), which pleas to God to hear the prayers that the Church is offering for you and your spouse and your future family. Your marriage will be a blessing to your children and to your neighbors. You are showing the world that love and commitment are possible. The Catholic community pledges to support you. The Church will pray for you during your wedding liturgy and will continue to do so throughout your married life.

Deciding to get married is one of the most valuable steps that you can make. Commitment is so important, not only for the validity of the marriage, but also for its success. Commitment provides safety and security, so couples can express their thoughts, feelings, and desires openly. When they're committed, they have the confidence that they'll make it through the day-to-day challenges and life's stressors that can tear a marriage apart.

You have chosen marriage, even while many couples choose to live together instead. The 2019 Census figures revealed that cohabitation is now more prevalent than living with a spouse.[5] According to the Catholic marriage website ForYourMarriage.org, currently 60 percent of all marriages are preceded by cohabitation, but fewer than half of cohabiting unions end in marriage. Some common reasons that couples cohabit include convenience, financial savings, companionship and security, and a desire to move out of their parents' house. Many couples believe—mistakenly—that cohabitation will lower their risk of divorce. This is an understandable misconception, since many people are the children of divorce, or have other family members or friends who have divorced.[6] Their desire to fully and freely give themselves to one another is a good thing. The problem is that their domestic partnership lacks the "all in" commitment of marriage. Although cohabiting couples may be sincere in their intentions, marriage demands a total and definitive gift of persons to one another.

As you continue to prepare for marriage, make an honest assessment of your reasons for marrying. If you are living together already, take time and space for reflection and prayer about your relationship.

Couple's Conversation

1. The Church is praying for you. Why is your decision to enter into a sacramental union important to the Church? What does the text above reveal about the purpose of marriage?
2. Why did you decide to marry?
3. Why do you wish to marry in the Catholic Church?
4. If you are already living together, why did you choose to live together?
5. What did you learn from the experience of living together?
6. If you are living together, are you open to refraining from sexual activity until you are married.

5. Currentz, Benjamin, "Living with an Unmarried Partner Now Common for Young Adults," U.S. Census Bureau, November 15, 2018, www.census.gov/library/stories/2018/11/cohabitaiton-is-up-marriage-is-down-for-young-adults.html; accessed August 20, 2019.
6. "Cohabitation," For Your Marriage website, United States Conference of Catholic Bishops, Washington, DC, www.foryourmarriage.org/cohabitation/; accessed August 20, 2019.

Chastity

Our sexuality is integral to who we are as humans, beings who are made in the image and likeness of God. The word *sex* comes from the idea of being "cut off." Adam experience loneliness before God made him a partner, Eve. Built into our human nature is a yearning for connectedness, for community, and for love. We have a sense, expressed so poignantly in the story of the first couple, of the sadness of being separated from God and from one another. We have a powerful drive to reconnect, to be in relationship with a loving other, to get back to the Garden of Eden.

The power of this sexual drive requires self-discipline, a virtue we call chastity. Every person, married or single, is called to be chaste. Chastity is not the same as celibacy. It comes from the Latin word for "pure," not just in sexual behavior but also in the sense of being "whole" or authentic before God, life, and relationships. Like courage, temperance (self-restraint), and honesty, the virtue of chastity is a habit of performing good actions according to a moral standard. When we practice the virtues, we strengthen them and thereby make the presence of God more and more visible in the world around us. St. Paul in his Letter to the Philippians captured the idea of virtue and the living of a virtuous life: "Whatever is true, whatever is honorable, whatever is just, whatever is pure, whatever is lovely, whatever is gracious, if there is any excellence and if there is anything worthy of praise, think about these things" (Philippians 4:8).

The virtue of chastity cannot be understood merely as a list of dos and don'ts. Purity is a grace that enables us to come to know, understand, appreciate, and accept our sexuality as a dimension of our whole being and so integrate it into our Christian life. Married people practice chastity by faithfulness to one spouse and openness to life in their lovemaking.

Chastity is evident in a person who respects the dignity of others and behaves responsibly about sex. Our interactions with all other people—not only with a spouse in marriage—will be holy and appropriate if we understand and practice this. Chastity guards a husband or wife from straying into inappropriate friendships that could harm their marriage. It helps a person have "custody of the eyes" on the internet and in public. A chaste spouse has no use for lewd conversation or pornography. Married people need to live in a network of friends where they will be supported in chaste living.

If sexuality is appreciated in its full meaning, Jesus is truly our model for healthy sexuality and chaste living. While Jesus was celibate, his single state did not negate his human sexuality. Jesus teaches sexuality in the context of covenant relationships. We become who we are in how we relate to others. In his life, Jesus teaches us that love and sex are not always the same thing. He enjoyed relationships that were intimate, faithful, equalitarian, and selfless, without genital relations.

Couple's Discussion

1. What challenges to chastity have you noticed in society?
2. How will you practice chastity in our married life?
3. Who are the friends you can count on to support your desire to be chaste?
4. What can you do to grow in chastity?

Children and Family Planning

In a marriage, the two of you freely consent and affirm that yours is a mutual, loving relationship in which you promise lifelong fidelity. Before receiving your consent to marry (the vows) the priest (or deacon) will ask you very specific questions: whether you are able to "enter into Marriage" freely and "without coercion," whether you will love and honor each other until death, and whether you are open to children. Your response to these questions ("I have / I am") should be truthful and honest.[7] These questions and answers publically and ritually declare your intentions to enter into marriage validly and sacramentally. Before God and the whole Church (represented by your family, friends, and others present) you declare your love for each other and the fact that you are open to having children together (if possible). As part of the sacrament of marriage, a couple is to be open to having children.

Parenting is hard work, but spouses can choose how they will respond to the challenge. In the process, each person can gain maturity and each can grow in appreciation of the other's developing abilities.

Children are thus truly the supreme gift of Marriage and contribute greatly to the good of the parents themselves.

—*The Order of Celebrating Matrimony*, 3

Catholic tradition's decision-making process can help a couple discern when to start their family and how many children they will welcome into their marriage. This means talking honestly, listening with your heart, consulting Catholic teaching, praying for God's guidance and strength, and trusting that God will be with you. Sometimes, a child is on the way before the parents feel that they are ready. Sometimes, one or both of them already have children before celebrating their marriage, or they are merging families.

Sometimes pregnancy is not possible, or they suffer miscarriage, or the couple is beyond child-bearing years. Although some medical treatments that respect Catholic values are available, not every couple will be able to have children. Still, the marriage of a couple who is not able to have children remains a sacrament. Whether or not they become parents, all spouses are called to have a fruitful marriage and share their love with the world. If their situation allows, they can welcome children through adoption or foster-parenting. They can also experience the fruitfulness of family life in a broader sense which includes aunts and uncles, cousins, relatives of relatives, and friends.

Whether you have biological or adopted children, becoming a parent will change your marriage, but you can trust that God designed your marriage to grow and deepen through that change. Caring for children brings with it the opportunity for parents to discover God working in their own lives. This is good news that people today do not often hear. Young parents today face an enormous amount of peer pressure to focus on the needs and desires of their children, even

7. *The Order of Celebrating Matrimony*, 60.

to the detriment of their couple relationship. Child rearing is such an important task that many couples find their lives consumed by it. Little energy is left for their marriage. Saving adequate amounts of energy for your marriage will pay off for your children in the end. They will have the security and role model of adults who are a strong parenting team.

The Church encourages married couples, within their means and the needs of their children already born, to be generous in welcoming children into their families. God gives people children to make them richer, not to make them poorer.

The Catholic Church teaches that marital intimacy, in order to reach its fullest potential to bond and unite the couple not only with one another but also with God, should never be deliberately isolated from its procreative nature. Since all forms of artificial birth control remove the possibility of conception from the act of marital lovemaking, they are not an option.

The Church understands that couples may sometimes have very serious reasons for spacing or limiting the number of children. In those times, the Church recommends the use of a Natural Family Planning (NFP) method, which limits intercourse to the times during the woman's cycle when she is not fertile. Your diocese will most likely require you and your fiancé to take part in a separate training session on NFP. What follows is a basic overview.

Sometimes couples face serious difficulties living in accord with this teaching of openness to new life. The Church understands and encourages all couples to find support in prayer and not lose confidence in the mercy and love of God. With the guidance of experienced instructors, couples learn to recognize and appreciate the natural signs of the woman's fertility. Using this knowledge, the couple can also use NFP. to increase the likelihood of conceiving. Your parish or diocese will help you sign up for a class on NFP.

Natural methods of family planning are based on female biology. During each cycle, a woman naturally becomes fertile as ovulation approaches, then infertile. The male, on the other hand, is always fertile. The woman's body gives her signs which indicate whether she is fertile or infertile. The primary signs for her are changes in the cervical mucus secretions before ovulation and the rise in basal body temperature after ovulation. Couples can learn to observe and record these signs and use the information for family planning.

A couple's motivation determines how effective NFP will be in helping them avoid pregnancy, if that is their intention. Studies have shown that NFP is at least as good as the barrier methods, (condom, diaphragm, and so on) and can be as effective as the pill when used by motivated couples.

> Your wife like a fruitful vine
> in the heart of
> your house;
> your children like shoots
> of the olive around
> your table.
>
> —Psalm 128:3.

If couples are going to practice NFP harmoniously, they soon find that they have to communicate more fully with each other and practice abstinence creatively. They do not ignore each other at times when they choose to avoid intercourse; rather, they develop alternative and non-genital ways of expressing their love.

Couple's Conversation

1. Do you want children?
2. How many children would you like to have?
3. How do we intend to plan our family?
4. Do you both agree on this method?
5. How are you going to deal with infertility if you are unable to conceive?
6. Are you open to adoption or foster parenting?
7. If you have children from previous marriages, how will you relate to them?
8. How will your parenting methods compare with your parents' methods?
9. Who will be responsible for nurturing, disciplining, bathing, changing diapers, and helping with homework? Will you have a shared approach?
10. Who will stay home from work with the children if they are sick?
11. Will one of you be a stay-at-home parent? Will you both continue to work? And if so, what form of child care will you provide?
12. What do you see as the joys and challenges of parenting?
13. What will you do to make your marriage relationship a priority for your family?
14. What important decisions are you facing as you begin your married life?
15. What issues do you agree about? What do you disagree on?
16. Who will you turn to for guidance?

Session 3

Financial Management

Liturgical Connection

When you consent to be married before God and before family and friends, you agree to journey together through all that life brings you—all "the joys and the hopes, the griefs and the anxieties."[1] Recall the opening discussion on the meaning of marriage. Marriage is a sacrament, a covenant, promise, and a commitment. Pope Francis emphasizes that one's true wealth is in their relationship with Jesus, not in money. The love you have for each other is intertwined with God's love for the Church. As a Christ-centered relationship, your marriage will be your true wealth.[2]

I, N., take you, N., for my
lawful wife/husband,
to have and to hold, from
this day forward,
for better, for worse,
for richer, for poorer,
in sickness and in health,
to love and to cherish
until death do us part.

—*The Order of Celebrating Matrimony*, 62 (Exchange of Consent)

Christian View of Money

Money in marriage is connected to communication, spirituality, intimacy, and health. Both parties need to be involved in the finances. Newly married couples find that financial issues can be some of the most difficult issues they face. Handling money brings up a lot of issues—your willingness to work with each other, to trust each other, to understand each other and the power struggles that may come with figuring out how to spend money.

As you prepare for marriage in the Church, in what ways can you focus your relationship to become a living holy temple in which space is created for the Word of God and Christ's presence is allowed to be central, more important than money or things? Of course, you will want to be able to have an income to provide for yourself and your family. But should money be your sole focus? Jesus would certainly say no. The Gospel is clear that one's focus should not solely rest on acquiring goods and money in this life, but rather striving to work for God and to build up a treasure that will be fully realized in heaven. This involves not trying to accumulate wealth here on earth, but if one does acquire wealth, to share it with others (see Matthew 6:19–21, 24). There is a reason why you never see a U-Haul trailer behind a hearse: you cannot take it with you!

But you may be wondering about being able to be comfortable in your married life together. You will certainly want to work towards financial stability and to be free from debt. The reality in our modern world is that we live in a transactional society in which money is needed to be able to provide for one's well-being. But Jesus tells us not to worry about material things (see Matthew 6:25–33). It takes a leap of faith to live into this vision for life. By seeking first the kingdom of God, we are invited to use our God-given gifts to build up the world around us. While doing so, there is a promise that God will indeed provide. This is certainly a daunting proposition to live into! By placing your trust in God, you have the opportunity to be freed of the anxieties and doubts that can creep in when thinking about finances. If you and your spouse are able to do so, however, it can be quite freeing and life giving. Go on; take the leap and place your trust in God!

1. *Pastoral Constitution on the Church in the Modern World (Gaudium et spes)*, 1. This is a document of the Second Vatican Council.
2. See Pope Francis, General Audience, August 7, 2019; available here: www.catholicnewsagency.com/news/true-wealth-is-found-in-jesus-christ-not-money-pope-francis-says-33446; accessed March 14, 2020.

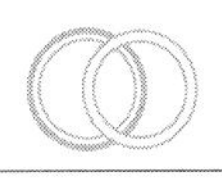

Managing Finances

Open and honest communication should also include financial discussions. No matter how much you love your spouse, trying to merge your lives—and your money—can be an enormous challenge. One of you may be a saver and the other a spender. You might be embarrassed about how you've handled money in the past—for example, by accumulating a lot of debt—and would rather your future spouse did not know about it. The way your family of origin handled money also influences the way you look at money. Although there is no one way to manage money in your marriage, there is a right way—the way that best suits the two of you after reflection and discussion.

> Let your life be free from love
> of money
> but be content with what
> you have.
>
> —Hebrews 13:5

How you spend, save, and plan the use of money—together—will have a strong influence on how well you are able to fulfill your promise to be true to the other, "for better for worse, / for richer, for poorer."[3] Arriving at a united perspective and approach toward money is challenging, but consider yourselves to be on the same team. Here are some helpful ways to negotiate this important part of your lives.

1. Establish a plan together.

Finances are often the biggest cause of stress in marriage. And we know that stress is a major cause of disease. Establishing a financial plan together will help you meet your financial goals and help improve your personal health. Write out the plan and periodically review it to make sure you are following the principles you have established together and are meeting your goals. As a living document, just like your body, the plan needs constant nourishment and adjustment. Money should be closely monitored to avoid miscommunication. Set a time each month to review your progress. You're in this together!

2. Set a budget.

The word *budget*, like *diet*, can have negative connotations. You might picture yourself living without, using coupons and denying yourself extras. But a budget can be very beneficial as a simple and flexible system that allows you to live within your means while keeping track of money earned and money spent. Budgeting will help you to

- Get the most out of your money.
- Plan for setbacks and take advantage of good fortune.
- Make wiser financial decisions.
- Become aware of how much and on what you are spending.
- Help you reach designated goals.
- Help your dreams become a reality.
- Prevent arguments and miscommunications about money.
- Protect you from yourself when you are at your weakest.

3. Save.

No matter what stage you are at in your marriage—newlywed, mid-life, retirement—it is always difficult to put aside money for the future. However, saving for eventualities is an important part of money management. It is wise to take advantage of the retirement plans your employer provides. The contribution is taken from your paycheck before taxes and is usually matched up to a certain amount by your employer. Starting young gives you time to compound the amount and prepare for retirement.

No matter how small, start a savings program for your marriage. Open a savings account at the bank and contribute a set amount each month. This gets you into the savings habit and shows that you really can save if you have the desire. Saving money always comes down to using self-discipline, which will help you implement a savings plan and curtail impulse spending.

3. *The Order of Celebrating Matrimony*, 62.

Here are some practical ideas for saving:

- Before you pay the bills, pay yourself first. Try setting aside a certain amount or percentage of each paycheck to go into savings.
- Save your income tax refund.
- Save a gift, a raise, or a bonus.
- Sacrifice one social event a month, and save the money you would have spent.

4. Embrace your gifts.

Embrace the talents you each bring to the marriage. Successful couples don't try to change each other—this just causes fights and tension. Use your gifts, talents, and strengths to be financially successful and achieve open communization. If you spend and the other saves, capitalize on these talents. Instead of seeing it as a liability, how can it be converted to as asset? The key here is instead of judging each other and working against each other, find ways to work together.

Managing Debt

Most people carry some form of debt, at least a mortgage payment, student loans, or wedding bills. Many people often live paycheck to paycheck and rarely have a reserve to fall back on in case of hardship. Some have never had to do without in their lives, and it can be difficult to begin a new life together when your immediate expectations are set upon the kind of home, care, or lifestyle it took your own parents a lifetime to achieve. Debt can creep up on us if we are not careful and can create many problems and strains in a marriage. Couples should be conscious of debt, for poor credit can affect future investments such as buying a home.

Here are some helpful tips for managing and preventing debt:

- Focus on your love and family instead of upgrading technology, buying bigger homes, better cars and clothes, and impressing others. You family is what's important.
- Avoid buying on impulse. Give yourself twenty-four hours to decide if you really want an item.
- Be on time with credit card payments, otherwise you will be charged a late fee and your interest rate can be raised. Late fees also damage your credit score, which affects your ability to purchase a home or a car with a lower interest rate.
- Calculate interest charges. Remember that if you don't pay off the purchase in full at the end of each month you are spending more money in the long run because of interest charges.
- Pay off credit card balances at the end of each month.
- Only use credit cards for emergencies.
- Explore student loan payback options, consolidation, and forgiveness (for example, those who work for non-profit companies may be eligible for complete loan forgiveness).
- Explore your options for filing taxes, whether it is filing as married jointly or separately. Filing jointly can cause issues with student loans, especially if you or your spouse is on an income-based repayment plan. Refer to the IRS website www.irs.gov/newsroom/correct-filing-status.
- When buying a home, research various loan and mortgage options for first time buyers, including Federal Housing Administration (FHA) loans.
- Prepare for the unexpected.

—Continued on the next page.

- Make sure your spouse is protected under life and health insurance plans. If both individuals have health insurance with their employers, it might be better (financially) to change your individual health plans to a family or self-plus-one-plan.
- Designate life insurance beneficiaries.
- You might fill out a medical power of attorney and an end-of-life form.
- Prepare a will.
- Be sure you have the proper education and training to protect your livelihood.
- Be open and honest, and communicate regularly about financial issues.
- Center your marriage on Christ and Gospel values.

Warning Signs of Financial Trouble

- Materialistic and self-centered (individualistic) views
- Rarely paying off a credit card balance
- Buying items on impulse
- Tring to justify a purchase by telling yourself you deserve it
- No money set aside for emergencies
- Retail therapy
- Borrowing from friends and family
- Borrowing in advance of your paycheck
- Spending a raise or a bonus before you receive it
- Setting up your whole budget around debt
- Using credit cards for necessities like groceries and taxes
- Not being able to pay off your credit card balances in full each month

Good Stewardship

When two Catholics marry, it is the Church's preference that they marry within a Mass. Sharing the Eucharistic is one of the primary expressions of unity that takes place within the marriage liturgy. The Eucharist, our great prayer of thanksgiving to God, is an encounter between God and his people. Likewise, when a couple and their guests share the Eucharist together, it becomes a visible expression of this unitive act.

During the Liturgy of the Eucharist, the priest will pray for the needs of the couple: "For those you created out of charity / you call to the law of charity without ceasing / and grant them a share in your eternal charity."[4] God so loved the world that he created humanity. And in this great love, he gave his only son so that all he created would be brought into deeper relationship with him and enter his eternal kingdom. Couples are called to model this great love God has for his people through acts of love, charity, and justice.

Think of your own participation at Sunday Mass. Before the Liturgy of the Eucharist and the sharing of holy Communion, the collection is offered. The money that we work hard to earn is given to the Church to be used for the needs of the poor. Just like Christ offered himself for our

4. *The Order of Celebrating Matrimony*, 201.

salvation, we too offer ourselves that we might become a living sacrifice of praise to God. This is what you are called to do as a married couple . . . to give of yourself. This act is not an isolated act between you and your future spouse. It is an act to be shared with the Church and with the world.

Within a marriage, you are called to good stewardship. Stewardship, in a Catholic, religious context, means that you are entrusted with a great responsibility. God has given all peoples the great gift of his creation. And God has given you a great gift with your love. Your call, your vocation or mission in marriage, is to share this gift with others and to be responsible for safeguarding his great creation in whatever means are possible.

Here are some practical ways that you can be good stewards with your finances:

- Use your financial resources wisely.
- Help others by giving of your time, talents, and money.
- Give out of your whole livelihood, not just of your excess or surplus.
- Set aside a portion of your income to give to your parish community and other charitable organizations.
- Donate goods such as food, blankets, toiletries, towels, and clothes for the poor.

Couple's Conversation

1. If you or your future spouse makes more than the other, is this an area of concern? Is the person with the higher salary more responsible for financial contributions?
2. What is your credit score?
3. What are your current debts?
4. What is the maximum amount each of you can spend before consulting the other?
5. Who will pay the bills?
6. Who will oversee investments, savings, and paying for current or future education?
7. Have you ever declared bankruptcy?
8. Do you owe money to family or friends?
9. Do you have a savings account?
10. Will you own or rent your home? Or save for a future home purchase?
11. Will you buy or lease a car? Will each of you have your own car?
12. Will you have a rainy-day fund? How much will you save each month?
13. Does your employer offer retirement benefits? If not, how will you prepare for retirement?

Continues on next page ▶

14. Will you keep money on hand for impulsive or frivolous purposes? How much will you keep on hand?
15. What is your view on cash versus credit?
16. If you will place your future children in day care how will you pay for this service?
17. Will your future children go to public or private school? And if private, how will you pay for their education?
18. What options do you have for life and health insurance?
19. Will you open a joint account? Will you maintain individual accounts?
20. What are your immediate and long-term goals for financial security?
21. What do you think of this statement: "Whatever financial resources I bringing into this marriage will remain my own." How much will you donate to charity? to your parish community?
22. How will your life together abide by God's "law of charity without ceasing"?
23. How will you show gratitude to God—and to each other—for what you have?
24. How will you give back to society for what God has given you?
25. In what other ways can you serve if you are having financial issues?

Budget Worksheet

Monthly Income and Deductions		Wife	Husband
Gross Pay	Wages and Salary (from paystub)		
Less Gross Pay	State Income Tax		
	Federal Income Tax		
	Social Security		
	Medicare Tax		
	Health Insurance		
	Life Insurance		
	Dental Insurance		
	Flexible Spending Contribution		
	Retirement Plan Contribution		
	Other Payroll Deductions		
Net Pay Total			

Some of these expenses may not be deducted from your gross salary.
If not, you will need to budget for these expenses from your net pay (take home amount).

		Wife	Husband
	Other Income		
	Other Money Received		
Net Pay plus Other Income			

Monthly Expenses	Wife	Husband	Total Budget	Actual Total
Home				
Mortgage or Rent				
Association Fees				
Property Taxes (usually with mortgage)				
Insurance				
Home Owner's or Renter's				
Additional Insurance Fees				
Utilities				
Water Bill				
Gas Bill				
Internet/Cable				
Phones (cell/landline)				
Auto/Transportation				
Car Payment				
Car Insurance				
Taxi/Ride Share/Public				
Fuel				
Licensing/Registration				

Continues on next page ▶

Monthly Expenses	Wife	Husband	Total Budget	Actual Total
Debt Payments				
Student Loans				
Credit Cards				
Other				
Discretionary				
Clothing				
Food				
Toiletries and Cosmetics				
Grooming (hair, pedicure, etc.)				
Memberships (gym, etc.)				
Household Products				
Car Maintenance (oil change, tires, repairs)				
Home Maintenance Costs				
Eating Out				
Entertainment				
Pet Fees (food, veterinary care)				
Child Care (including day care, alimony, etc.)				
Child's Education				
Savings				
Savings Account				
Emergency Fund				
Education				
Retirement				
Travel Account				
Gift Giving				
Contributions				
Parish Donations				
Other Charitable Donations				
Total Expenses				
Net Surplus or Loss (Income less Expenses)				

Mandatory expenses are those you have commited to pay, such as a mortgage or utillity payments. This means you have signed a lease or have received a loan and are required to pay a set amount each month.

Discretionary expenses things are those you need or want but you have a choice as to how much you spend.

Session 4

Communication, Conflict Resolution, and Reconciliation

Liturgical Connection

At the end of the Mass—and your wedding liturgy—the priest sends the assembly out on a mission. It is an instruction, a command. In these simple words, the Church communicates to God's people the purpose of our Christian life: to be like Christ!

When you participate in the liturgy, whether it is Mass or another form of prayer, it will engage all of your senses. You see the color of the vestments, the smoke of the incense, the ministers in procession. You hear the prayers, the readings, and the music. You offer prayers, you talk in dialogue with the priest, and you sing the music. You smell the aroma of the incense. You touch other people at the sign of peace. You might hold the Eucharist in your hands. You taste the consecrated bread and wine. You feel the emotions of the psalms, and you might be moved to tears by particular petitions for those in need. Your body moves in procession, kneels in sorrow and penitence, and stands in joy.

> Go in peace, glorifying the Lord by your life.
>
> —Dismissal at Mass

The liturgy is sensual! Through your entire body, God communicates to you through Jesus. Jesus Christ is our great communicator. Through the liturgy, Christ is present to you and communicates God's love to you. You are graced—even kissed!—with God's embrace of mercy. With the many signs and symbols of the liturgy, God engages your senses to fully experience and encounter Christ's presence and understand the great mystery of our faith.

Your partner is probably a mystery to you. Little by little, he or she reveals more about their personality, their interests, and their dreams. With every touch, every move, and every word, your spouse will open themselves more fully to you and allow you to encounter them in an honest and truthful way. In order for marriage to flourish, grow, and adapt to change, open and honest communication must take place within a marriage. Your communication with one another must be Christ-like. Just like in the liturgy, how you interact with your spouse is a reflection of your love of God and helps the other encounter the holy.

Healthy Communication

Marriage is a covenant, a sacred promise between the two of you and God. No partnership can survive or flourish if the partners don't communicate with each other. You are probably aware of the failure rate of friendships or businesses that have failed because of poor communication between the parties. This is true for you in the covenant promises you've made in marriage. Communication is the dialogue that keeps the covenant alive and growing.

It is no secret that we do not always communicate with others as well as we should. Throughout your marriage, and especially in these early moments of your life together, it is important that you establish patterns that will help you communicate clearly and in love, even when you disagree with each other. Each of us has different gifts, talents, and life experiences that lead us to communicate in the ways that we do. Be mindful that the very thing that is causing you to be annoyed with your loved one might be a talent or gift you have not yet recognized in him or her. Be attentive, too, to the ways that your fiancé was raised, the ways his or her parents or family communicate with one another, and the effect of unresolved conflict within his or her family,

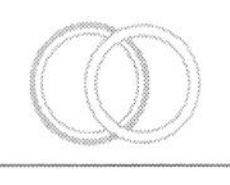

as these will all have bearing on the way you learn to share your thoughts, feelings, hopes, fears, and experiences together.

Good communication is intimate. When you think of intimacy in a marriage, more often than not, sexual intimacy comes to mind. Intimacy involves more than a physical expression of closeness. Intimacy also involves how you communicate with one another—your body language, your facial expressions, the tone of your voice, and the way you touch your beloved.

To achieve intimacy in your marriage communication, it is necessary to be vulnerable and speak in a language of feelings. Sharing feelings allows you the freedom to avoid judgements and accusations, and to concentrate on the unique connection between each other. Sharing your feelings enables each of you to discover the uniqueness in each other and will draw you even closer, both physically and emotionally.

Feelings can involve both anger and joy. While you may be reluctant to express yourself out of fear of what might transpire, withholding your feelings denies your identity. It presents a false image to your partner and can build individual resentments.

Practice Effective Communication

- Set aside fifteen minutes a week to practice the communication tips listed above. At first, this may feel forced or awkward, but over time you will strengthen the ways you communicate with each other.
- Begin by sharing something your fiancé did in the past week that you especially appreciate, and talk about the experience together. Following a few conversations about pleasant things, address more uncomfortable ones—a time you have been disappointed or frustrated with something your fiancé did.
- As you become comfortable with the skills listed, apply them in real time, when something comes up that needs to be addressed, either positive or negative.
- At first, you may need to have the points of effective communication listed on an index card or memo on your phone. Soon, these skills will become second nature to you!

Couple's Conversation

1. When do you communicate best with your partner?
2. What settings or moods help you reveal your innermost thoughts and speak honestly about yourself and your feelings?
3. What strengths do you bring into the marriage?
4. Are you a good listener? How can you improve your listening skills?
5. What do you believe are your gifts? How can they help you improve your communication skills with your spouse?
6. What are your partner's gifts and talents?
7. Does something your partner does annoy you? How might you reframe these annoyances as gifts?

Effective Communication

Effective communication does not happen overnight and requires equal participation from both people. Here are some ways to help you communicate better:

1. Be an active listener.

Listen twice as hard as you speak. There's an old saying: There is a reason God gave you two ears and one mouth. Refrain from interrupting, and ask clarifying questions before you answer.

2. Be careful with non-verbal communication.

Gestures and body language can send powerful messages to each other. Sometimes a gesture might seem normal to you but be completely misunderstood by your spouse. When this happens, your gestures might need to be explained.

> Listening is already an act of love!
>
> —Pope Francis

3. Be clear and succinct.

Less is more. No need to go on and on to make a point. Avoid jargon or technical terms. This can create a sense of superiority and condescension.

4. Clarify.

Be certain there is mutual understanding of the issue. Ask more questions where doubt remains.

5. Be vulnerable.

Be vulnerable and open with each other. Allow yourselves to know each other's feelings and innermost thoughts. This is a pathway to healing.

6. Build trust.

Trust is built over time and can be one of the most fragile elements of a relationship. It is far better to be truthful. Dishonesty always reveals itself.

Breakdown in Communication

A lack of clear and compassionate communication can become a barrier in your marriage. When there is a breakdown in communication, you might witness the following:

1. Your partner appears not to be present.

We've all seen it at some point: in the middle of a discussion, we look at our loved one and see a nodding head, glazed eyes, and a general state of disinterest. Glazed eyes are generally not a good sign.

2. You keep getting the same question.

There will always be questions—and that's a good thing in terms of discussion and engagement. Questions themselves aren't an issue. It is an issue if you're consistently asked to elaborate on critical information that you have discussed from the start.

3. You keep repeating yourself.

Perhaps you are giving too much information. We tend to "tune out" when a message seems to go on and on and lacks clarity. Less is more.

4. Fear

Protecting each other's feelings is a normal part of marriage. Fear can restrict your openness and willingness to convey true feelings. Avoid barriers by trusting your partner and his or her ability to help with healing.

5. Avoidance

We can become exasperated when attempting to share our inner self. Feelings of rejection can cause us to choose an alternative path when communicating. "It's easier than having another argument" is not a good solution for the issues that enter a marriage. Face them head on, driving to closure.

Communication in the Digital Age

We live in a digital age, where shortened text messages and emojis have become normal and acceptable ways to communicate. Because communication has changed so much over the last few decades, it is important to give special attention to social media and how it can affect your marriage. Social media can be a source of positivity and building community. Your activity on social media should always be affirming toward your significant other—never hurtful or critical—and always be used in a trustworthy manner. The following tips will help you use social media in an appropriate way.

1. Keep everything in the open.

If you don't have a joint husband/wife Facebook account (or other social media platform) make sure what you say online is nothing you couldn't say with your spouse standing there beside you. Before messaging, ask yourself, "Is this something I wouldn't mind my spouse seeing?" You may even consider letting your spouse read it first. It's good for accountability, and it's a good way to double-check that what you've written isn't miscommunicating what you meant.

2. Say what you need to say, and say it to the right person.

Rather than gripe about a marital problem on social media, talk directly with your spouse. If you think it might hurt feelings or get you in hot water, think of a way you can soften the blow when you raise the issue. In most cases, the following approach is helpful: "I know you care about me, and I know you probably didn't think about it, but I feel (insert your emotion) when you (insert the offense). I don't want problems to build that will isolate us. Can we work through this together?"

3. Use social media to build each other up.

It's never been easier than it is right now to send a note to each other for no reason at all or to brag about your spouse in front of others. Social media makes it easy to connect with each other while you're apart during the day, and that will keep a relationship from drifting. Just make sure that what you say online is reinforced by what you say and do when you see each other in person. (And be sure not to post embarrassing pictures of the other spouse without their permission.)

4. When you're together, come together.

It's very easy, even when you're home, to drift to your own individual social media corners. By the end of the evening, you realize that you've hardly spoken a word. This happens with parent-child relationships, too. Set your personal devices aside, and plan some face time (the real thing, not the Apple product.)[1]

Couple's Conversation

1. What is the place of social media in your life at present?
2. Do you ever catch yourself posting something you know may not be comfortable or appreciated by your fiancé?

1. This list was compiled from an article written by Scott Williams and published in the online publication FamilyLife. It is available here: www.familylife.com/articles/topics/life-issues/challenges/media-and-entertainment/4-ways-to-avoid-being-a-social-media-marriage-casualty/; accessed December 9, 2019.

Conflict Resolution

It's good to begin all communication with the belief that underpins your marriage. Your marriage is a covenant, a promise. You are a team; your mission is to form a partnership of love and life. When conflicts arise, you are not opposing quarterbacks, but one team trying to reach the goal line together.

Every couple argues. You will not always agree on which goal you are pursuing and how to get there. There are five basic issues that almost every couple disagrees about at some point in their marriage: time, sex, money, children, and in-laws. Couples that stay married handle their disagreements differently than couples that divorce, even though they have the same number of conflicts. Disagreements are a sign that there are two intelligent and unique people in a discussion. It's not the disagreements that ruin a relationship but the way those differences are handled.

> Put on, as God's chosen ones,
> holy and beloved,
> heartfelt compassion,
> kindness, humility
> gentleness, and patience,
> bearing with one another
> and forgiving one
> another.
>
> —Colossians 3:12–13

Here are ways to handle a disagreement:

- Pick your battles.
- Remain calm and confident.
- Be respectful, courteous, and polite.
- Focus on the important issues.
- Stick to the issue at hand.
- Be honest and explain how you feel.
- Take responsibility for your part in the situation.
- Sometimes you just need to take a deep breath and take a break.
- Try to find humor in the situation.
- It's ok to cry.
- Compromise and negotiate.
- Accept each other's flaws.
- Try to understand the other's perspective.
- Touch your spouse (positively and lovingly).
- Apologize.
- Follow up if you need to.
- LOVE!
- Pray together.
- Always see the other as Christ.

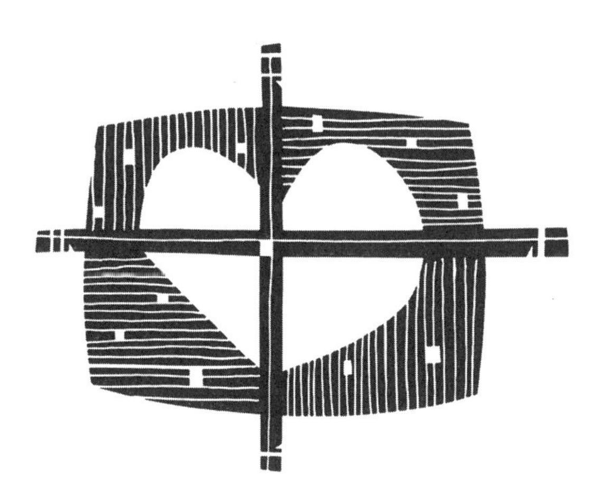

Here are some important things to avoid when faced with an argument or conflict. Try not to:

- Win.
- Interrupt.
- Argue over trivia.
- Preach.
- Change the subject.
- Avoid excuses.
- Yell, shout, or be sarcastic.
- Use the word "*but*".
- Blame.
- Call your loved one names, swear, or use other foul language.
- Use accusatory statements.
- Give the silent treatment.
- Walk away.
- Go into the "man cave."
- Bring up old incidents.
- Generalize.
- Jump to conclusions.
- Exaggerate.
- Criticize or become exasperated if your spouse cries.
- Use words such as *never, always*, or *must*.
- Bring up someone else's opinion about your spouse.
- Compare your spouse to another family member.
- Embarrass your partner.
- Show contempt for your partner's ideas.
- Disregard your partner's feelings or ideas.
- Laugh at your partner or make fun of him or her.
- Argue in public or in front of children.
- Vent about your spouse on social media.
- Post passive-aggressive memes or comments on social media.
- Bash your partner to a friend, family member, or colleague.
- Deliver an ultimatum.
- Go to bed angry.
- Refuse responsibility.
- Threaten divorce.
- Fight when drinking—sober up first.
- Throw things or use any form of violence (emotional or physical abuse).[2]

Closure in Arguments

The primary goal for any conflict is closure. Closure will allow both of you to move on and be confident that the same subject will not come up again.

It is important to differentiate between problems and issues. Conflict is often defined as a problem. Before you know it, you are overcome by seemingly never-ending problems. Foundationally, problems reside in the core building blocks of a relationship—trust, respect, fidelity, honesty, and so on. When these important aspects of marriage are fractured, they look like issues. Issues need to be much more well defined. Isolating the issues and focusing on solutions allows for a much more effective process for closure.

Generally, when conflict presents itself, it is emotional. Allow for the toxic influence of hyper emotion to dissipate, and approach the situation calmly. Consider agreeing on a "code word" to be introduced when emotions become unchecked and a break is necessary. The word or phrase is known only to you and your spouse and will only be used when appropriate. It is not to be used as a weapon for control. Both of you have the right to invoke the "code" and give each other a break.

2. If there is any hint of abuse in a marriage, seek help immediately. Refer to page 63 in this resource.

When returning to discuss, if emotions are still high, reset again.

Process for Closure

These steps will help bring closure to an argument or conflict. This is not an exercise in creating a win-win solution, but a *winning* solution. There are no gold stars or win/loss columns for your marriage.

1. Define the issue.

Be detailed and specific.

2. Individually admit how each person has contributed.

Be open and honest with personal shortfalls.

3. Use "I" statements.

When expressing how you feel, it is important to do so from the first-person perspective. "You" statements can be interpreted as accusatory and might make your spouse feel defensive.

4. Identify past attempts.

List your efforts at resolution that have been unsuccessful.

5. Brainstorm.

Make a list of possible solutions for solving the problem (no more than ten). It is important not to judge or criticize your spouse's suggestions.

6. Evaluate the suggestions.

Discuss each suggestion, and allow emotion to have a voice. Be objective.

7. Agree on one solution.

Pick one possible solution to try. This may or may not be the one that fixes the problem. It is a starting point. If it fails, you still have nine more to try!

8. Be invested.

List how you will each support the solution. Be specific, and accept the solution. Avoid the "I told you so" or "it will never work" excuse if the solution fails.

9. Progress.

Set another time to meet to review the solution, and make adjustments where appropriate.

Practice Closure

After a time of disagreement, either immediately or later when you have both had time and the emotional ability to discuss what happened, use the list above to help you process what happened, and come to closure about it. This is another time when such discussions might feel awkward at first, but over time this will become natural to you, and your relationship will benefit from your honesty and vulnerability.

Serious Threats to Marriage

In a Christian marriage, you promise "to be faithful . . . to love . . . and to honor . . . all the days of [your life.]"[3] These promises take work, commitment, and respect. In order for a marriage to work, you should reflect on your vows regularly and make a conscious effort, each and every day, to uphold and cherish these promises. Sometimes

3. *The Order of Celebrating Matrimony*, 62.

these promises are broken. It is good to be aware of the serious challenges that can threaten your marriage and which would require outside counseling assistance. If any of these behaviors are affecting you, your spouse, or your family, please seek help through Catholic Charities, counseling services, or your parish. Don't give up on your spouse to any of these negative behaviors. Fight for his or her heart and for the marriage as you treat the disease. In some situations, such as with emotional and physical abuse, it may be difficult to overcome. It is the Christian perspective to reconcile and forgive. However, that does not mean you are required to remain in an abusive environment or if your or your children's safety is at risk.

1. Abuse

Spousal abuse can be sexual, physical, verbal, mental, or even financial. No form of abuse has any place in marriage. You may see it as a loss of control on the part of your spouse when it is the need for power and control to dominate the other person. Embarrassment often prohibits one to talk about it even with close family members and friends. This unwillingness to confide in anyone is partly the result of feelings of shame—a certain social stigma attached to abuse. True for any form of abuse, the first step to recovery is ownership by the abuser. Always seek professional assistance. The behavior will not cure itself. If you or a family member is a victim of abuse, it is important to seek help immediately. More information about abuse is found on page 63.

2. Infidelity

Why do partners cheat? Humans are social beings, and we are hard wired to seek happiness. Over prolonged periods of abandonment and rejection, we attempt to self-medicate by filling the void of sadness with support from others. *This is not to say that it is the other spouse who is at fault due to a lack of attention or emotional support.* True, it can be a contributing factor; however, few people wake up in the morning and say to themselves, "Today, I am going to cheat." Catholic teaching is clear that infidelity is adultery (one of the Ten Commandments), and infidelity includes desire, or an emotional affair. "Adultery is an injustice. [One] who commits adultery fails in his [or her] commitment . . . [and] does injury to the sign of the covenant which the marriage bond is . . . [and] compromises the good of human generation and the welfare of children who need their parents' stable union."[4]

3. Alcohol, Drug, or Substance Abuse

Drugs and alcohol can destroy a marriage easily as a partner chooses drugs or alcohol over spending time with a spouse. Many issues of trustworthiness, resentment, and sexual detachment are symptoms often related to this form of abuse. Denial is often the first line of defense for the person suffering with this dysfunction. It is common for spouses to blame addiction on the other person when the real blame lies with the disease. One must be on guard not to enable. Twelve-step treatment programs are available, such as Alcoholics Anonymous (AA), your parish community, Catholic Charities, hospitals and medical clinics, counselors, and other service organizations.

4. Pornography

Pornography is an epidemic worldwide, especially because of the internet. Without leaving home, a person is just a few clicks away from explicit and violent sexual content 24/7. Even though most pornographic content is viewed by men, an increasing number of women are now using it. The use of pornography not only objectifies the other spouse (and women and men in general), it introduces a third person into the relationship. Pornography is a form of adultery and infidelity. Medically, we know that prolonged use of this media creates an even deeper desire for more. Pornography is addictive in very much the same was as drugs and alcohol. Catholic teaching is very clear that the use of pornography "offends against chastity because it perverts the conjugal act, the intimate giving of spouses to each other. It does grave injury to the dignity of its participants

4. *Catechism of the Catholic Church*, 2381.

(actors, vendors, the public) since each one becomes an object of base pleasure and illicit profit for others."[5] If you are struggling with an inclination toward or an addiction to pornography, there is help for you. Resources are available at www.pornharms.com.

5. Technology

Our technologically driven world is a gift and a tribute to the intellectual capacity of humanity. Technology has increased productivity, made many tasks much simpler, and provided easier access to increased knowledge. At the same time, it has its risks. Too much time is spent glued to screens and playing games. Technology can be used as a tool to facilitate harassment, control, and abuse. Cyber bulling is just one example which has had severe consequences. This portal also provides easy access to other abuses like pornography. Much like any attraction, moderation is important.

Conscience

Conscience is an interior voice that prompts us to honestly assess our behaviors, recognize the negative effects of our choices, desire to change our hearts, and return to God. With God's grace, we can change behaviors that keep us from God and hurt our relationships. Grace is God's help to do things that are not possible with natural human capacities alone. We all fall short somehow of our own ideals; grace helps us become the kind of person we want to be.

Having a well-formed conscience involves studying the best information available as a critical starting point. For Catholics, this will include learning what the Catholic Church teaches about a given issue.

Sometimes people face serious difficulties living in accord with Catholic teaching in sexual matters. The Church understands and encourages all to find support in prayer and not lose confidence in the mercy and love of God. We have a duty and obligation to seek after the truth as much as we can, to seek the wise counsel of the Church, of those who can point us in the right direction.

In marriage and family life, people are called upon to make decisions about life-changing issues. Catholics have a process of decision making to help guide them in moral questions as well as in practical matters.

Process for Making Good Decisions

- Identify your needs and wants. These may not be identical.
- Define the desired outcome. What do you want the end result to be? Do you agree on what you want?
- List the alternatives. Is there another option? Can you wait to decide?
- Gather information. Get all the facts about the subject at hand—as much information, from as many sources as possible.
- Evaluate. Weigh and compare the accumulated information, and list each fact as a pro or con.
- Discuss honestly. What does each of you expect the outcome of this discussion to be? What does each person think and feel is important?
- Pray about your decision. Pray throughout the entire process, separately and as a couple.
- Make an informed decision. Once you have thought it through, you can make the decision with confidence.
- Share with your spouse. Tell each other what you have decided. If your decision is not the same, begin your discernment process again.
- Review your decision periodically. As time goes by, you may decide differently, or you may affirm your choices.

5. *Catechism of the Catholic Church*, 2354.

Examining Your Consciences

The sacrament of reconciliation, also known as Penance or Confession, helps us examine our consciences, and the act of confessing our doubts and fears can help us become more forgiving. The sacrament of penance is an opportunity to encounter the God of mercy through the person of Jesus Christ. Conversion of heart is also accomplished by daily prayer, gestures of reconciliation, care of the poor, and regular examination of conscience.

Going to confession before your wedding is an excellent idea. If it has been a while since your last confession, do not worry. The priest will be happy to listen to you, forgive your sins in the name of Christ, and extend God's grace to you. An examination of conscience to use when preparing for the sacrament of reconciliation is found on the next page.

Personal Examination of Conscience

- Am I able to choose what is right and good?
- Am I committed to what I know is right?
- Do I accept both my goodness and my shortcomings?
- Do I stand up for my beliefs in all areas of my life?
- Am I aware of my basic need for and dependence on God?
- Am I sensitive to the hurt and pain of others?
- How willing am I to share hurts with someone else?
- Am I willing to remain calm in the midst of hurt, anger, and confusion?
- Am I able to accept my need for forgiveness and recognize God's gracious mercy?
- Am I willing to forgive when someone has wronged me?

Forgiveness and Reconciliation

When conflict occurs, as it undoubtedly will during your life together, remember your wedding vows (or your consent to marry). Before you exchange consent to marry, the priest or deacon will ask you, "Are you prepared, as you follow the path of Marriage, to love and honor each other / for as long as you both shall live?"[6] After agreeing to do so you will then "promise to be faithful" to your beloved "in good times and in bad, / in sickness and in health" and "to love . . . and to honor [your beloved] / all the days of [your] life."[7]

To be *faithful* means more than promising not to have any other partners. You are promising to *keep the faith* in your marriage, to believe in your joint vocation to be a sign of God's faithfulness in the world. You are vowing to stay connected, whatever challenges come into our lives. You are on your spouse's side. Aim to keep the lines of communication and respect open between you.

To *love* means to actively seek the good of your spouse, to look beyond their shortcomings and see the beautiful person that God created. Think about how God, your good and loving Father, has forgiven you for your own mistakes. Love like God loves you.

To h*onor* means to esteem and treat another with respect because of who they are. Sometimes the word "cherish" is used in place of "honor," but the meaning is the same. Practice holding yourself and your partner in warm regard, even when feeling distant or during a fight. Consider how you would like to be treated, then treat your spouse that way. Continue treating one another the way you did when you were dating and first fell in love. Be polite. Hold the door for your spouse. Say please and thank you. Listen well. You honor your spouse when you live up to your commitment to love them, even when they occasionally are not acting very loveable.

When you are wrong, admit it and apologize. When you are right, don't gloat. Authentic apology means taking responsibility for your actions and

6. *The Order of Celebrating Matrimony*, 60.
7. *The Order of Celebrating Matrimony*, 62.

making a commitment to change. Speak respectfully, even when angry. Avoid the silent treatment or cutting humor. Eliminate disrespectful behaviors such as rolling your eyes, interrupting, or talking negatively about other people. Everyone deserves to be heard, even if you don't agree with a person's views or opinions.

Forgiveness cannot be demanded or rushed. No one should be pushed to forgive before they are truly ready. Forgiveness is a process, and several steps may need to occur before they are ready to forgive, such as talking about your feelings, trying to understand the other person's point of view, and accepting that you have been hurt. Aim to repair damage in the relationship and stay connected so that love can grow.

> **Be kind to one another, compassionate, forgiving one another as God has forgiven you in Christ.**
>
> —Ephesians 4:32

Steps to Forgiveness

- Ask yourself: What is the problem?
- Make sure you are hearing what the other is saying and that they are hearing you.
- Ask God to grant you insight into the other person's motivations.
- Decide if you are ready to say you are sorry or to accept the other person's apology.
- If you don't feel ready to forgive, you may need more time to think about what happened.
- Does the person appear to feel sorry for what they did? If not, it may be harder to forgive. In this case it may be a good idea to seek some advice from a trusted counselor.
- If you are ready, say, "I'm sorry for . . . ," or if the other person apologizes say, "I accept your apology."
- Commit to intentional action to address your partner's needs and concerns.
- Make up—reconcile—with your spouse.

Demonstrate your desire to reconcile after an argument by owning up to your mistakes instead of dwelling on them. Look for opportunities to move past them, and do better next time. Don't make excuses. Let go of anger, and be willing to change. Recognize that you're not perfect and that there are areas where you (and your partner) need to improve. Swallow your defensiveness, and make the effort to follow through. When your partner sees that you take their concerns seriously, they will be more likely to feel valued and respected. This can create a positive cycle in which they appreciate you and feel more loving towards you.

Couple's Conversation

1. Who or what really presses your anger buttons? How do you deal with it?
2. Give an example of forgiveness that has inspired you.
3. What do you think "turning the other cheek" means?
4. What can we do when it is hard to forgive?
5. Remember a time when you found it hard to forgive. Share the story and the outcome.
6. When is it acceptable not to forgive?
7. Think of someone who has held a grudge. How did refusing to forgive effect that person?
8. What part does God play in our being able to forgive one another?

Session 5
A Life of Prayer and Discipleship

Liturgical Connection

On the day you enter into the sacrament together, some of the last words you will hear during the liturgy will be the final solemn blessing prayed over the two of you by the presider:

> May God the eternal Father
> keep you of one heart in love for one
> another,
> that the peace of Christ may dwell in you
> and abide always in your home.[1]

The text speaks directly to the heart of your spiritual life together. Let us call to mind who God is—this is important for exploring what it means to have a spiritual life. Over the centuries, Christians have wrestled with how best to understand who God is. The author of the First Letter of John writes, "God is love" (1 John 4:8). The type of love that is used in this passage is a particular type of love that is other-focused. It is a love that is unconditional; it seeks out and truly wishes what is best for the other, regardless of circumstance.

When you marry, the two of you will be uniting your individual lives into one married life together. This will entail a sharing of different aspects of your lives in a new and exciting way. Your physical lives, your emotional lives, your mental lives, and your familial lives, to name a few aspects, are all components of what makes up the fullness of the entirety of your life together. One really important aspect that you will be able to share with each other, in an even deeper way than you already may be doing, is your spiritual life.

What is a spiritual life? Your spiritual life refers to the deepest meaning and values that you have in your life. How you begin each day, how you reflect upon the day that has past, how you look toward the future, and how you honor your past, are all connected to your spiritual life. It speaks to how you are connected to God and therefore with others. Your spiritual life is central to your existence as a human being. As you enter into marriage together, how you bring your individual spiritual lives and blend them into your marital spirituality will have great bearing on your marriage.

You enter into the bonds of marriage as equal partners. Each of you has been given great and unique gifts and talents by God. First and foremost, you will have the opportunity to share these directly with your spouse. Serving one another in an authentic way that truly works for the betterment of the other will help strengthen what you have together. Taking a stance of service for your beloved allows you to truly be "of one heart in love for one another," and this will continue to strengthen

1. *The Order of Celebrating Matrimony*, 77.

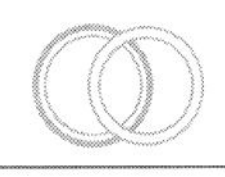

your marital bond.[2] This can then affect the world around you in a really positive way!

It is important to recognize the mutual partnership that exists within your relationship. One does nor lord over the other, but rather the two of you enter into your marriage covenant as equal partners who will share in the work of keeping that one heart in love alive and well for each other.

Second, taking an active part within the life of the Church will help you both be open to Christ's peace dwelling within you.

Here are some ideas:

- Being a part of a faith community allows us to be attentive to Christ's Word proclaimed so that it can inform our daily living.
- Attending Mass together offers connection with Christ present within the Mass and the Church community; you can then go forth to share what you receive during Mass with the rest of the world.
- Look for ways to get involved either in your local parish or within a parish that feels like home for you. Seek out ministries in which you can make a difference in the lives of others, and in so doing, you will find that you yourselves get nourished as well.
- Seek out a small faith community that can support you in your growth as a couple. Perhaps your parish will have something organized to connect with other married couples. If your parish does not offer something like this, check with your diocesan family life office to see if they can help you connect with a local small faith group.
- If you have children, being connected with a Church community will in turn help foster their own spiritual growth and development. Being actively involved in a parish community will definitely help strengthen your growth as a family.

By finding a community of faith and actively anchoring your marriage within that community, your spiritual life as a married couple will undoubtedly become more grounded in Christ's presence in your lives.

Third, be connected with the world around you. As you are being formed yourselves within a Church community, you can then, in turn, help share the Good News with others around you, even by just how you are living your lives. The way you engage with others in the various circles you inhabit can go a long way toward sharing Christ's peace with others. We will explore this more in the next section.

2. *The Order of Celebrating Matrimony*, 77.

Couple's Discussion

1. What has your own spiritual development been like up until this point? Do you consider yourself to be a spiritual person?
2. Do you consider your future spouse to be a spiritual person?
3. Who were some people in your childhood who influenced your spiritual development? What did you learn from them? How did they affect the trajectory of your spiritual life?
4. How does this passage from scripture resonate with you: "God is love" (1 John 4:8)?
5. Why did you choose to get married in the Catholic Church? Was that a difficult decision to make together?
6. If you had any hesitation on choosing to get married in the Church, how did you resolve that hesitation?
7. How is your relationship in regard to power dynamics?
8. Is one of you more dominant within your relationship, or do you approach your relationship as mutual partners?
9. What has you own experience with being involved in Church been like up until this point?
10. What parish ministries, programs, service projects have you had the opportunity to explore up to now?
11. What has been your experience as a couple in Church-life been like?
12. What is your perspective on being part of, and active in, a faith community?
13. What do you think your partner's perspective is on being part of, and actively involved in, a faith community?
14. What are some areas of parish life that you feel you could get more involved in?
15. What are some parish opportunities that you'd like to explore getting more involved in with your future spouse?
16. How can your involvement with a faith community help strengthen your relationship with your partner?
17. What is your individual prayer life like right now?
18. What is your prayer life together, as a couple, like at this moment?
19. How can you explore placing a greater emphasis on your prayer life together?

A Life of Prayer

One extremely important step that can be taken to help develop your spiritual life as a married couple is to foster a life of prayer together. To borrow the words of Venerable Patrick Peyton, "The family that prays together stays together."[3] Prayer is an essential part of our Christian lives as it helps us be aware of God's presence among us and helps us deepen our relationship with him. For married couples, prayer also helps make Christ the center of their marriage and helps the couple be Christ for one another, especially in challenging situations. And while prayer allows us to communicate directly with God and to be aware of his presence, it also changes our hearts. The popular bumper sticker that reads "Prayer changes things" might more accurately read "Prayer changes people, and people change things."

Newly married couples learn the importance of making prayer a priority in their lives, especially when they face some of life's challenges such as sickness and death, the loss of a job or a broken relationship, or struggles with infertility or miscarriage. They also learn the importance of praying to thank God at times of great joy such as a job promotion, the birth of a child, or when a loved one receives a clean bill of health.

Couples will find benefit both in praying together and alone. While praying together as a couple is praiseworthy, it is just as important to set aside time for individual prayer. Prayer time can be formal, using traditional prayers like the Our Father or the Hail Mary, or prayers that are spontaneous and from the heart. Even spending some time alone with God in silence can be effective. Just as a couple gets to know one another more and deepen their relationship by spending time together, so too prayer gives couples a golden opportunity to spend time with God and each other and also to deepen their relationship with him and each other. When both spouses have healthy prayer lives on their own, there is a greater chance that they will have a healthy prayer life as a couple.

An important part of an individual's or couple's prayer life is praying for the needs of others. We can pray for loved ones who are ill or for people we don't know across the street or across the world facing hunger, persecution or any other life situation. Praying for others reminds us that we don't live in isolation.

Mass

The centerpiece of the prayer life of married couples should be the celebration of Sunday Mass and honoring the day of the Lord's Resurrection not simply by having a day of leisure and rest but by entering deep into the heart of the mystery of Christ's dying and rising, which we do at every Mass. Mass is the most important thing we do each week, not just the fulfillment of an obligation.

3. Information about Fr. Peyton can be found at www.fatherpeyton.org.

It gives us strength and nourishment to get through our week.

Making the Sunday celebration of the Eucharist a priority in the life of a married couple presents a challenge in our society, where people often work more than one job or work extra hours at their regular job to support themselves or to prepare themselves financially for when they have children. Sporting events, leisure activities, catching up with family and friends, and a genuine need for a healthy balance of exercise, rest, and sleep also take up time on the weekend.

> The Eucharist is the source and summit of the Christian life.
>
> —*Dogmatic Constitution on the Church*, 11

It is very important for couples to block the time for Sunday Mass on the calendar so it becomes a priority rather than something extra to fit in. Some couples find that a routine can help make Mass a priority. For example, Saturday or Sunday late afternoon Mass can be followed by a special dinner. If Sunday morning Mass works better, Mass can be followed by breakfast or brunch out or a special breakfast made at home. It may take a while to find a routine that works, so couples should be patient. And of course if and when children become part of the family, the routine will naturally change.

Some couples find that participating in a liturgical ministry helps them connect to the Mass more deeply and keeps them in a routine. Couples could even serve together in ministry as readers, extraordinary ministers of holy communion, ushers, greeters, or choir members. Many parishes welcome the ministry of young married couples and will likely give them some flexibility with scheduling, knowing the many demands that are placed on their schedule.

Prayer at Different Times of the Day

Praying before meals is another traditional form of prayer that can be adopted by couples. A simple sign of the cross or the more formal traditional meal prayer "Bless Us, O Lord" are appropriate before eating. Couples need not be embarrassed about praying a prayer aloud in a restaurant or public place. Being mindful of those who are without food is an appropriate consideration.

The beginning and end of the day are appropriate times to pause and thank God for the time that has passed and to ask for strength in the time ahead. Many couples find they are more comfortable with informal prayer at these transition times of day while others find that more formal prayer, even from the Church's official ritual of Morning Prayer, Evening Prayer, or Night Prayer are best for them. These times of prayer consist primarily of psalms, a hymn, a brief scripture passage, intercessions, and responses and take only about ten-to-fifteen minutes to pray. There are several apps available that allow people to pray using their mobile devices—for example, when they are commuting to or from work.

Eucharistic Adoration or Holy Hour

Spending time in the presence of the Blessed Sacrament outside of Mass is an important element in fostering a relationship with Christ. This can take place in one of two forms: adoration in front of the tabernacle, which can be done any time the church building or Blessed Sacrament

Chapel is open, or during Eucharistic Exposition, when the consecrated host is exposed in a monstrance for public devotion, usually during set times of the week or month in a parish.

Praying with the Scriptures

Praying with the scriptures is a beautiful way to spend time with Christ. Individuals or couples could read one or more chapters of scripture at a time or focus on one or two key sentences or phrases. Praying with or meditating on key passages of scripture is an ancient practice of the Church and is referred to as *Lectio Divina*, or Holy Reading.

Having a Bible in the home is a good idea. A larger and more beautifully designed family Bible could even be out in a common area and used for more formal prayer while a smaller study Bible could be kept at the bedside or on a nightstand for quicker reference. It might be helpful to write notes in the Bible itself or in a journal. Passages related to the time of year could be read individually or as a couple. Some people have a custom of keeping memorial prayer cards from the funerals of significant people inside the family Bible.

The Rosary

Many couples find consolation in praying the Rosary either individually or together. This ancient prayer form, which can be prayed anywhere or anytime, uses beads to help count the Hail Marys and consists of contemplation on five particular events called *mysteries* in the life of Christ. There are four different sets of mysteries (glorious, joyful, sorrowful, and luminous) that are used on different days of the week. Each mystery is accompanied by a *decade*, which consists of an Our Father, ten Hail Marys, and a Glory Be.

Silence

Sometimes being alone without any formal or structured prayer is the best way to pray. Silence invites the one praying to speak directly to God and also for God to speak to the individual. Notice that the words *silent* and *listen* include the same letters in a different order. In creating a prayerful space free of distractions, silence allows space for the one praying to listen to God. This is very important, especially at times when an individual or a couple is discerning God's will about career paths, relationship situations, when or where they should purchase a home, or whether or not the time is right to welcome children into the marriage.

Participating in Parish Life

Married couples are encouraged to participate in the life of their local parish. You might consider attending part of a parish mission or a Lenten soup supper, or you might avail yourselves of the sacrament of penance. Perhaps there is a scripture study class or other form of adult faith formation that might be beneficial to your prayer life. Your parish might have some type of forum or group for newly married couples. You might even want to serve as a liturgical minister; often couples join choirs together or serve as extraordinary ministers of holy Communion. Check the parish website, Facebook page, or bulletin. If nothing exists, consider suggesting it to the pastor; however, be prepared to be involved in leading the group if you suggest it.

Home Rituals

There are many traditional Catholic rituals intended for use in the home or the "domestic Church," as a Christian home is often called. Some rituals are related to various family situations, such as birthdays and anniversaries, news of pregnancy, or the beginning and ending of the school year. Others are related to the Church seasons, such as the Blessing of the Advent Wreath and the Christmas Tree and the blessing of food on St. Joseph's Day and Easter. If there are young children in the family, they will love being involved in these prayer services and can even take part in reading the scripture or even leading the prayer when they get older. *Catholic Household Blessings and Prayers*, published by the United States Conference of Catholic Bishops, contains these traditional prayer rituals and also has a treasury of Catholic prayers every Catholic should be familiar with.

An Environment for Prayer

Finding a comfortable place conducive to prayer may take some time and experimentation. Some couples are more comfortable praying outside with nature, while others find peace praying inside the home, perhaps even in a small area set aside for prayer. Still others prefer to make a visit to a church or chapel. Go wherever you and your spouse can find Christ. Sometimes a lighted candle, crucifix, holy image, or statue provides a focal point conducive to prayer.

Couple's Conversation

1. Why is it important to attend Mass regularly as a couple?
2. Did you have particular rituals that you celebrated growing up? either at home or at church? Are these rituals that you would like to incorporate into your marriage?
3. What are some obstacles you have to praying?
4. How can your home reflect the importance of prayer in your lives? Is there a space for an open Bible and perhaps a candle?
5. Do you rely only on traditional prayers, such as the Hail Mary and Our Father, or have you brought your troubles and joys to God in prayer spontaneously?
6. How could you begin to bring your concerns as a couple to your prayer life?
7. Have you prayed with the aid of a liturgical calendar so that you could ask for intercession of the day's saint?
8. What time of day would work best for you to pray as a couple?
9. Have you ever just talked to God about your day as a form of prayer?
10. Could you establish a quiet time of ten minutes for you and your spouse to just sit quietly with God as a form of prayer?
11. Have you ever prayed with a passage from scripture?

Discipleship

By entering into a Christian marriage, the two of you become witnesses to God's love in the world. Being in a committed and loving relationship in which each person is wholly dedicated to the other really does run counter to much of our modern day culture. Through forging a relationship together that truly wants the best for the other person, you are able to be an embodiment of Christian love in the world. Your marriage does not become an end unto itself, only looking in on itself. Rather, it is something that is shared with the world, helping to bring forth the kingdom of God.

By placing God at the center of your marriage, you have the opportunity to be formed in God's love, which in turn allows you to go deeper in love with your spouse. Flowing from the love that you share in your marriage, you can then authentically share that same love of God with a broken world that so dearly needs it. By your marriage, you can be an echo and embodiment of God's love throughout the world.

How might this become fully realized within your life? Through your baptism, you have become a disciple, a follower, of Jesus Christ. In joining together in marriage, the two of you have the opportunity to make discipleship a principal aspect of your marriage, together. In baptism, Christ has called you to follow him; in marriage, you will have the chance to respond fully with your spouse. Now let us not be naive; discipleship is not always easy. In fact,

> May you be witnesses in the
> world to God's charity,
> so that the afflicted and
> needy who have
> known your kindness
> may one day receive
> you thankfully
> into the eternal dwelling
> of God.
>
> —*The Order of Celebrating Matrimony*, 11 (Solemn Blessing)

it is usually quite difficult. Jesus even talks about the challenges of following him when he says, "Whoever wishes to come after me must deny himself, take up his cross, and follow me. For whoever wishes to save his life will lose it, but whoever loses his life for my sake will find it" (Matthew 16:24–25). These verses come right after Jesus is talking about the great trials that he himself was going to be facing in his life on the road to the cross. As disciples, we too will face hardships in authentically following him. The road of discipleship can be rocky and challenging.

This challenge of discipleship exists for everyone who is a follower of Christ, but a real blessing in Christian marriage is that the two individuals who unite together in marriage have an exciting opportunity to journey together as disciples in following Jesus. Flowing from baptism, your call to discipleship takes on a new dimension through marriage, in which each of your calls to following Jesus can be united along a common avenue of discipleship. Christian marriage actually is discipleship, when you think about it; for in the sharing of the sacrament together, you ground your love for each other within God's love. As a result, you have a partner with whom you can work together to follow in Jesus' footsteps and live out his teachings.

Here are some ideas to help you with discipleship:

- Make it a point within your marriage to make Sunday the highpoint of your week together. Attend Mass together, and be attentive to the Gospel proclaimed within the liturgy. Allow the Word proclaimed and the homily shared to influence your daily living as a married couple.
- Prepare ahead of time for Sunday Mass by breaking open the Sunday readings as a couple and sharing your thoughts about what you read and how it affects your lives. Listen attentively to the message that you are reading and to what is being asked of you through scripture.
- Spend some time volunteering together in a place where you can make a difference in lives of others. Make it a point to reach out in kindness to the "afflicted and needy" who can benefit from your positive impact as a married couple trying to do good for others. Find a particular cause that both you and your spouse are passionate about, and make a commitment to it.
- Allow prayer practices that work for you as a couple to guide your way in discerning how best to engage the world around you.
- Keep a focus throughout your married life on loving God, loving your neighbor, and sharing the love that you have for each other by serving the world.

Couple's Conversation

1. How does God's love help shape the love that you have for your partner?
2. Can you identify connections between God's love and the love you share with your beloved?
3. Share your thoughts about the following statement with your partner: Marriage is an echo of God's love.
4. Think about your own baptism (if you are a baptized Christian). What do you think are some of the responsibilities that come along with having been baptized?
5. What are some of the difficulties that you face in being a disciple of Jesus Christ?
6. What are some of the joys that you've experienced in being a Christian disciple?
7. How might you and your future spouse be able to partner together in your common discipleship through your marriage?
8. Explore some opportunities for volunteering with your partner. Which ones seem like viable options for the two of you to dedicate some energy towards?

Prayerful Exercise: Writing a Love Letter

Work on this exercise at home after participating in your formation day.

You are encouraged to pray together to strengthen your bond and to grow together in faith and love. As a way to strengthen your commitment to one another, take some time to write a letter to your fiancé. Think of this exercise as one of the ways in which you are praying for the other.

Today, letter writing is almost a lost form of communication. Computers, tablets, smart phones, email, texting, and Instagram give us immediate access to each other, no matter where we are. While this is a quick and convenient way to communicate, you can't be sure how what you say will be interpreted. Saying how you feel, why someone is important, and speaking as one lover to another demands reflection, deep thought, and the right choice of words.

Writing a letter to your fiancé will help you probe deeper into your feelings and thoughts about your future spouse. Writing will help you share emotions you might otherwise be reluctant to say aloud. The letter is a statement of what your relationship looks like.

Appendix 1
Special Considerations

Communicating with In-Laws and Parents

When you were baptized, you became adopted sons and daughters of God. Everyone who is baptized is part of God's family. Much like your own family, God's family is on a journey together. We share each other's joys and hopes, and ups and downs. We all share the journey of life and are hoping that, one day, we will all be fully part of God's kingdom.

In Catholic liturgy, this journey is symbolized by the many processions that take place—the opening procession of ministers, the procession with the *Book of the Gospels*, the procession with the gifts of bread and wine that will be offered and become the Body and Blood of Christ, the procession to receive holy Communion, and the procession at the end of Mass into the world. A liturgical procession is a metaphor of the journey we make together as Christians. We are all part of God's family, moving toward a common goal—entrance into the kingdom of God. The procession is a holy sign of our journey toward union with God.

You might be surprised to know that what you've probably experienced before at weddings isn't exactly what the Church envisions for how this should take place. The directions for celebrating the wedding say, "The procession to the altar . . . takes place in the customary manner."[1] This means that the procession is to model what takes place at Sunday Mass! The procession may be led by a server carrying incense, a cross bearer accompanied by candle bearers, a minister holding the Book of the Gospels, and the priest(s).

What about the wedding party? The entire wedding party will be part of the procession. Remember that everything we do at the liturgy has meaning. You are about to become one with your new spouse in marriage, and you are making this journey together as a Christian couple, as God's children. But your family and friends are also part of this journey. And since the procession symbolizes the journey toward fuller relationship with God, they are also part of the procession. After the priest, the wedding party will process together. You might choose to process with your own parents, or your parents can process before you as you and your spouse walk in together, all while a song of joy is sung. This form of the procession is a powerful symbol of the two families who are supporting you, praying for you, and journeying with you in this public declaration of your love for one another.

> **Blessed are all who fear the Lord, and walk in his ways!**
>
> —Psalm 128:1

Think back to the exercise you did about your "Family of Origin" (see page 3). This exercise should have given you a sense of how both of you grew up, what traditions you celebrated, and how your families dealt with challenges. You may have shared similar experiences, or you might have been surprised to hear how your significant other grew up.

It is very important to understand that you come to this marriage with a unique set of family characteristics. You will enter your marriage with different values and ideals formed from your families of origin. These values and ideals have made each of you into the person you are today. However, you are now becoming a family of your own. This doesn't mean you forget about how each of you grew up. You should talk about what was important to you growing up and how you would

1. *The Order of Celebrating Matrimony*, 46.

like to integrate these values and traditions into your new family.

You will also want to develop new traditions that the two of you and your future children will share together. This doesn't mean you forsake traditions of the past. Introduce new things to your partner and try to share them together.

In marriage, you will establish new traditions and standards unique only to you. This merger of your past allows for your individuality while relying on your life experiences to clarify what you really want in your own marriage. Developing your own consensus will save you time and prevent arguments. Ideally, your decision will come about where both have an equal ownership and equal responsibility for the outcome. Like "conflict resolution," closure remains relevant when developing consensus. You should what to always present a unified message to others. Regardless of subject matter, the message is a strong affirmation to supporting one another.

Your extended family—parents, grandparents, sisters, and brothers—are also becoming part of your new family. In-laws can sometimes be challenging to any marriage. You should discuss how involved your family members will be in your marriage. The relationship you have with your extended family should continue to be respected and fostered. And you will need to have patience and compassion when helping your future spouse develop his or her relationship with them as well. Don't expect your spouse to be "best friends" with your own mother immediately. As with any relationship, it takes time, commitment, and patience to foster these relationships—and it can't be forced.

The conflict management section in this chapter will help you navigate the sometimes rough waters of in-law relationships. In addition, here is some helpful advice for journeying together as one extended family in God.

Here are some ways to help with in-law issues:

- Your priority is your marriage.
- Be supportive of your spouse, and maintain a "team" approach.
- Never criticize your spouse to your own parents.
- Spouses should manage the relationship with their own parents.
- Clear boundaries need to be established (especially with your children).
- How you celebrate birthdays, holidays, and other special traditions needs to be established in advance.
- Expectations should be communicated and be realistic.
- Try to put yourself in your spouse's shoes when problems arise, trying to see the problem from their perspective.
- Be open and honest with each other and with your own parents. Concerns need to be voiced, but be patient and understanding about the situation.
- Don't talk about politics.
- Try not to compare your spouse to your own parents. Your spouse is his or her own unique person with their own gifts, talents, and quirks.
- Relationships can't be forced.
- Always be kind. Keep a level head. Laugh!

Couple's Conversation

1. How will your family make time to start its own traditions and celebrate the holidays together while also making time for the extended family?
2. How will you stay in touch with your parents? Will it be mainly by visits, Skype, or phone? If they live close by, will you visit weekly, bimonthly, or occasionally, for instance on holidays, birthdays, and other events? If the parents live farther away, will you intentionally visit for holidays and other occasions or more often? Who will be responsible for keeping in touch with the parents? Will you periodically assess as a couple whether you spend a sufficient amount of time with each spouse's parents?
3. How much of a role do your parents expect to have in the wedding preparation? Have you and your spouse discussed whether you are each comfortable with their expectations? How can you discuss your desires for the level of the parents' involvement with them?
4. When you have children, do you have caretaking expectations for your parents? How will open communication be established regarding disciplining the children?
5. If your parents and spouse experience a falling out, how will you support your spouse?
6. Would you be willing to talk to your parents if your parents and they experience a rift?
7. Are there ways your spouse can help you be more comfortable at events with his family?
8. How does your spouse's family communicate differently than yours? Do you find their communication method difficult for you?
9. Are political discussions important to your own family?
10. How will you handle disagreements with how your children should be raised?
11. What are your parents' expectations for the religious upbringing of your future children? And how do you respond to these expectations?
12. Do your parents have any desire to name your future children? Do you think this involvement is acceptable?
13. Are you comfortable with your in-laws providing financial assistance?
14. Do you desire to live near your parents?
15. Will your parents have a key to your home? Are they free to access your home without permission?
16. How would you describe your current relationship with your future in-laws? Do you have concerns? Are there challenges that should be discussed before your marriage?
17. It can be difficult to accept the realities faced with aging parents—the financial needs, the emotional ups and downs, and the responsibilities with health and physical care as well as end-of-life plans can cause stress on any marriage. Are you prepared to handle these together in an open and honest way?

Multicultural Unions

One of the beautiful cultural adaptations that may be included in your wedding liturgy is the Hispanic tradition of the blessing and exchange of golden coins. Within this rite, called the Blessing and the Giving of the Arras, as the coins are exchanged with one another, the now newly married couple says to each other:

> **N.**, receive these arras as a pledge of
> God'sblessing
> and a sign of the good gifts we
> will share.[2]

This tradition, symbolizes in a visible way that in marriage each person brings within and offers to the other the good gifts of what he or she has and is as a person. From this mutual donation comes the common treasure that will establish the assets for happiness and common good. Couples that have different cultural backgrounds have abundant good gifts to share. However, using a symbolic language we can say that, since in an intercultural marriage each person's *arras* come in different "currency," the couple needs to deposit those treasures in the "Bank of Love," where each currency could be valued fairly so that the cultural differences will not impoverish but increase their mutual growth.

Our culture is part of what we are. It has to do with the traditions that mark our preferences when choosing what to eat, or what to wear at special occasions, and even on how to celebrate our faith or how to express love, happiness, or grief. Culture could also be the source of expectations about the husband's or wife's roles within the relationship, about how to manage the budget (and who does so), on the children's education, and the distribution of house chores. In few words, our culture determines how we live our daily relationship with others and in society.

With this in mind, it is advisable that multicultural couples be aware of their differences. Each person should not only respect the other's cultural particularities but also somehow find most of them agreeable. Consider that your fiancé's culture will soon be part of the traditions you, and your kids, will share as a family and with your in-laws.

Learning new traditions and enjoying them is not only fun. It will also expand your cultural experience and your capacity to interact with other people. Most of all, it will reinforce your union with the fruits of mutual admiration and understanding. It will create among you a new cultural synthesis where each one can learn new ways to enjoy, to celebrate, to express yourself, and to pray. Children from multicultural parents grow with the capacity to understand others' cultures and adapt better in today's world, which is also more global and multicultural. The Catholic experience of Christianity is also a call to a universal relationship with each other. Your cultural diversity is then an opportunity to live and celebrate at home the multiculturalism of the Catholic Church.

Accepting and embracing differences is not always easy. Our cultural identity may also be a source of tension or misunderstanding. In a good marriage, a couple overcomes the temptation of imposing "my way" or "your way" and instead looks together for "our common way." Because of this, when cultural differences become a source of conflict it is advisable to accept that differences are normal not only among intercultural couples, but in any relationship. Begin with an open mind, trying to understand and appreciate the other's cultural differences as something you have not yet discovered. Talk together about the moments you could celebrate, integrating some of each other's customs or the kinds of parties you would celebrate—for example, some sober-mindedly and others with loud music.

If a cultural attitude is contrary to your values, and against Gospel values (for example a "macho mentality"), this is an opportunity to help your partner discover new and better ways to live and love each other. However, culture does not validate being disrespectful. Explain openly and respectfully to your partner why that attitude is hurting you. Most of all, finding in the Gospel the

2. *The Order of Celebrating Matrimony,* 67B.

good reasons for changing some of our cultural bad habits or discriminatory behaviors will make the Christian culture of love your own culture. Only if you find that your fiancé's culture is contrary to fundamental values of your Christian faith, and that he or she is not open to learn and embrace your Christian values, should you consider not marrying that person. Remember, our faith is an essential part of ourselves, and cannot be negotiated.

To love is also to give the other person the right to be different. Because of that, stay open to accept that some cultural things may never be completely embraced by your spouse. Marrying one of another culture can be an adventure in which couples are invited to enter the fascinating world of the other person and enrich their lives with new traditions, customs, recipes, and ways of seeing and experiencing life. Your family will also become a new enriched space with the intercultural competency Christ proposed for the new saved humanity, where, as St. Paul described, it will no longer be "*neither Jew nor Greek, slave nor free person . . . for you are all one in Christ Jesus*" (Galatians 3:28). All of this could then happen if Christ's universal love is the source of your relationship.

Couple's Conversation

1. How does your culture celebrate Christmas, Easter, Mother's Day, Father's Day, Valentine's Day, funerals, birthdays, and special occasions?
2. How does your culture celebrate marriage? Who pays for what, and what kind of special traditions or rites and foods are used during marriage receptions?
3. How could you integrate all of these differences in your marriage reception?
4. What particular religious traditions did you grow up with (novenas, family devotions, and so on)?
5. What does your culture consider to be the role and functions of a wife and mother in a family?
6. What does your culture consider to be the role and functions of a husband and father?
7. In your culture, how do spouses usually share chores?
8. What does your culture think about stay-at-home husbands?
9. What does your culture think about a woman working outside the house?
10. How does your culture treat elders and children?
11. What kind of music do you prefer to listen to? and for parties?
12. What kind of traditions would you like to share with your future children?
13. Share about a great value you bring from your own family to your new family and how you would both like to adapt within your new family.
14. Share a negative value (experience) in your family that you do not want to continue in your new family. What is it, and why don't you want to continue it?

Marriage and Divorce

After great suffering, a new season is upon you. You've passed through many states of heart and mind—certainly pain, perhaps also numbness, outrage, disappointment, guilt, resentment, fear, brokenness, mourning, and more. You have reached a state of acceptance and hope, perhaps even peace, and readiness for the future. Now, after all that, new love and life have found you.

Whether you are new to the Church or a lifelong Catholic, you have experienced her resources in the annulment process. Through introspection and writing you have reviewed the story of your life and the story of your previous marriage yet again. You have reflected on it and received new insights about yourself and about how the Church understands marriage. Now you have a deeper sense of how a sacramental marriage could work—how the third person in your marriage, Jesus Christ, can hold each and both of you as you work through the days of married life.

Doubts may yet haunt you—What are you thinking? Your previous marriage failed—what makes you think this one can work? A spouse betrayed you before—how can you trust again? There are so many unknowns. If you have children, how can you help them grow into the new family you are forming? They may still be wounded and confused and need enormous patience and understanding from both of you. How can you know this is the right path? How can you know God is with you?

If you have come this far, you have already been praying and discerning—individually and together. You have reflected on your desires and your doubts; you have asked God for guidance, you have been open to promptings from the Holy Spirit. Perhaps each of you has talked with people who know you, people you perceive to have wisdom. Eventually you reached a calm center, an assurance deep within that you have been called to serve God as a married couple.

This discernment process, as individuals and as a couple, will be ongoing—a constant touchstone for you throughout your life together. Challenges and moments of darkness will visit you, as they do every person, and you will not know how to deal with them—they swoop in so fast! Caught up in the moment, you will find it hard to stop your racing mind and turn to your spiritual resources. But Christ will be there, loving and shepherding you, eager for you to open yourselves to him. The most terrible feelings or thoughts you can imagine will not scare him away or offend him. He knows the whole of us and the full spectrum of marital behaviors.

> **Our concern must be to know God's will. We must enter that path if God wants, when God wants, how God wants.**
>
> —St. Gianna Molla

Build on the spiritual tools you have already developed—prayer and scripture reading certainly, and also patient listening and reflection as you search, individually and together, for Christ's presence in every situation, for Christ's presence in each other. There is no one and only way to do this, but as many ways as there are individuals and couples. Find the ways that suit you. And know that this sacrament of marriage has the power to nourish and change you, little by little, into the partnered disciples whom Christ (and the world) need you to be.

Couple's Conversation

1. What are some of the doubts or concerns that linger as you anticipate remarriage?
2. What are some of the characteristics of your coupledom that give you hope and confidence in this marriage?
3. How will you keep yourselves aware and open to Christ's presence in your marriage? What spiritual tools and strategies will you develop—individually and as a couple—to help you turn to him?

Marriage and Step-Children

If you have been to Catholic Mass recently, you will probably recognize this prayer: "with all the Angels and Saints, we praise you. . . ." At every Mass that is celebrated, the priest will say a variation of this before everyone sings, "Holy, Holy, Holy, Lord God of might." If you choose to celebrate Mass at your wedding, you will hear this prayer.

When we celebrate the liturgy, we are united with the angels and saints in heaven. We are surrounded by their love, and in heaven, they sing the same praise and thanksgiving that we sing on earth at Mass. Think about this! What an amazing, cosmic reality! Through Christ, we are united with the halls of heaven! Humanity is no longer separated from God. We are all adopted sons and daughters of God, united together through Christ. This is what's called the marriage of heaven and earth and the Communion of Saints.

Praying through the saints is an important part of the Catholic tradition that is often integrated at Catholic weddings if the couple has a particular devotion—especially to the Blessed Virgin Mary. After the blessing and exchange of rings, there is the option to sing a hymn. This is the perfect opportunity to sing a song to the Blessed Virgin Mary.

Think about Mary for a moment. She was a young girl, probably around the age of thirteen, pregnant with the Son of God. She wasn't married when she became pregnant with God's child. But she became betrothed to a man named Joseph. We don't know much about Joseph from the scriptures. But we can surmise that he was a kind and faithful man, compassionate to the needs of this young girl, marrying her and taking in her child as his own. Traditionally, Joseph is referred to as the "foster father," "adoptive father," or "step father" of Jesus. This united family becomes a model of holiness. Pope Francis teaches that "every family should look to the icon of the Holy Family of Nazareth. Its daily life had its share of burdens and even nightmares."

The Holy Family, especially Joseph, is a great model for couples who are marrying and bringing children into their union. Think about Joseph's situation: he loved Jesus, a child that was not his own flesh and blood; he provided for Jesus' needs, his food, water, and shelter; he taught him skills. He took on this child's needs as his own, protecting him from the wrath of Herod.

Falling in love and finding the right partner is a time of great joy for a couple. When there are children from a previous marriage or relationship coming with you into this marriage, you will have challenges that will need your love and commitment to manage and overcome.

Whether the children are younger, or grown and out of the home, some of the dynamics listed below may be part of this new family's considerations.

- Unrecognized loss and unexpressed grief often underlay a step-family life.
- A step family takes about seven years to "cook" and come together well, and the honeymoon may need to wait a few years as the new couple hits the ground running.
- "Biology" not "step" is a bonding dynamic, so early discipline issues are usually best addressed by the biological parent.
- Children may resent the new member of the family and might make it very difficult for this person to feel welcome.
- Holidays may always be a struggle.
- Rituals need to be redefined and new ones formed.
- You have no control over your former spouse's choices.
- Treating the other parent with respect provides security for the children.
- Be patient and loving.

Couple's Conversation

1. How might the Holy Family, especially Joseph, be a model for your own merging family? What does he teach you about love? What inspires you about his story? How can he be a model for you in how you interact with your stepchildren?
2. How does it affect your faith—and your relationship with each other—knowing that the saints in heaven, including Joseph and Mary, are praying for you and guiding you as you make this difficult transition as one family?
3. Are you prepared to take on your future spouse's children and love them as your own?
4. Who has custody of the children? How much time will they be with you? How does this make you feel?
5. Who will be in charge of parenting and discipline decisions?
6. How will you help your new children understand that you are not trying to replace their mother or father?
7. Are you comfortable with your future spouse's interaction with his or her former spouse?
8. How will you interact with your future spouse's former spouse?
9. How will this interaction affect your own relationship with your new children?
10. Are you comfortable contributing financially to the well-being of your new children?
11. Are you aware that you will be faced with challenges immediately upon marrying? How do you think these challenges will affect your marriage?
12. Will you be patient and loving with any behavioral issues that might arise because of your marriage?

Marrying a Widow or Widower

"Until death do us part," is not as clear cut as it sounds when a widow or widower contemplates a second marriage. Spiritually and emotionally, the physical death does not end the relationship.

For a variety of reasons, marrying a widow or widower (at any age) is much different than marrying someone whose marriage ended in divorce. Reflect on the following differences. People get divorced because a marriage did not work out. With a widow or widower, the marriage in most cases *did* work. Those who lose a spouse in death and who choose to remarry usually have had a good experience of marriage. They are realistic about both the joys and challenges of married life. Depending on the length and experiences of the first marriage, your fiancé is hopefully more aware of the strengths and issues he or she brings to your upcoming marriage.

It's important to be aware of how your fiancé has integrated the loss of their first spouse into their daily life. Have they done their grief work so they are ready to move on to a new, freely chosen life with you? It is important to recognize that grief is a process. It is normal to experience grief after the loss of a loved one, even when falling in love with someone else. It is possible to grieve one person and love another simultaneously.

In a divorce, possessions are split. The former spouse takes their possessions with them. They are gone. But even years after someone is widowed, their first spouse's belongings may still be present. Your spouse's previous life is part of what you will marry into. The old adage that one marries their partner's whole family is even more expansive when marrying a widow or widower. It is not just the family of origin, but also the nuclear family of children, grandchildren, and perhaps former in-laws.

I . . . take you . . . to have and to hold . . . until death do us part.

—*The Order of Celebrating Matrimony*, 62 (Exchange of Consent)

Couple's Conversation

1. Learn as much as you can about stages of grief and what to expect. Read books about grief. Do some online research. Consider seeing a counselor for yourself if you have questions or concerns about your own feelings.
2. Discuss how and with whom you will celebrate different holidays.
3. Are there rituals your fiancé and his or her family remember the deceased spouse? How do each of you feel about your being included in those celebrations?
4. Will there be challenges to be faced as you enter into your fiancé's nuclear or extended family? How can you and your fiancé support each other through these challenges? Keep in mind if your fiancé's children or other family members struggle to accept you. It likely has nothing to do with you. It may be part of their own grief process.
5. Together take time to communicate about what things are up for compromise (where, who to vacation with) and what are not (time with children).
6. Discuss what kinds of new memories you can create. Are there new things you can do together? New traditions at birthdays or other holidays?

Marrying Later in Life

Marriage will always remain one of the biggest decisions of any person's life. It involves more than decisions about finances, faith, kids, and so on. When it comes to marrying later in life, people tend to take more time to discuss concerns and share real life experiences prior to making any long-term commitment. There are numerous advantages and disadvantages to waiting.

Financial stability often is much more relevant than at a younger age. People have experienced much and have often planned or even reached their financial goals. Connected to this is a well-defined career path and employment. With age, it can mean wiser decisions and an ability to properly prioritize a marriage. Maturity teaches us many things about life and helps us take much more well-informed decisions. We tend to have a better idea of what a relationship should be and have a good sense of what we are looking for.

Challenges? "This is the way I have always done it!" Flexibility can be strained when bringing together two "established" personalities. Battle tested and comfortable in one's routine, additional effort should be placed in marriage preparation. Each person has had an opportunity to experience firsthand self-reliance. Opening up to include another in their life journey will feel awkward at first.

Couple's Conversation

1. How will you combine expenses and assets?
2. What is your retirement plan?
3. Which healthcare plan will you keep?
4. Are you open to children? If you are not able to have children, how will you be nurturing in other ways? Are you open to fostering or adopting children?
5. Will you continue in your career?
6. How will you practice your faith together?
7. Are there any health issues that your future spouse should be aware of?
8. Do you have life insurance in place?
9. Will you rewrite your wills or write one for the first time?

Ecumenical, Interfaith, and Interreligious Marriages

Take a look at the prayer on the side of this page. It is an excerpt from the special nuptial blessing that is prayed over a Catholic who marries a person who is not baptized. It is clear from this text that the Church believes that the institution of marriage predates Christianity as well as Judaism, but came forth at the beginning of their creation. Marriage has long been part of social customs and practices in all cultures; however, Catholic teaching emphasizes that marriage belongs to God's creative acts and the order of nature and natural law. Humans, by their very nature, are social beings. And through God's grace, their union is sanctified and elevated to a holy status. The scriptures with an account of marriage (see Genesis 1 and 2) and define the salvation Christ's gives to all as the marriage of heaven and earth (see Revelation 19:7, 9). This is a powerful symbol!

Marital challenges have always existed, and these challenges have sometimes involved religious differences. Early Christians, reflecting on Christian marriage in light of their experiences of marriage within their diverse native faith communities, believed that marriage between two Christians took on an added dimension. Christ became the center of their union. Because there existed different traditions, "Christian" marriage involved many challenges. Some Christians married members of the Jewish community. Others married Romans. Their love was not bound to religious or political boundaries.

Still today, Christians marry those of other faiths. It is more and more common for a baptized Catholic to marry another baptized Christian but one who is of another denomination, such as Lutheran or Baptist. It is also common for Catholics to marry people who are not Christian but Jewish, Muslim, or Hindu. In some cases, Catholics might marry atheists or agnostics.

Perhaps this is your experience. Be assured that the Church recognizes the love that you and your future spouse share and rejoices with you at your upcoming marriage. She continues to pray for you and will be available to you for strength and support throughout your married life. In fact, the Church rejoices so much in your relationship, that she provides two forms of the wedding liturgy to accommodate your needs. Your pastor will help you with deciding from among the options.

Holy Father, maker of the whole world,
who created man and woman
in your own image
and willed that their union be crowned with your blessing,
we humbly beseech you for these your servants,
who are joined today in the Marriage covenant.

—*The Order of Celebrating Matrimony*, 139 (Nuptial Blessing)

All marriages involve some differences in faith, even if the two marrying share the same Catholic religion. No one's faith journey is the same. And we all mature and grow in this faith in different ways and at different times. Since we are unique individuals with various histories and backgrounds, our perceptions, understandings, and experiences of God, faith, and the Church will always differ. Couples marrying today, whether they are of the same religious tradition or not, face the same challenges as did couples two millennia ago.

Faith and our religious traditions are important elements of our lives to be shared, especially if you are marrying someone of a different faith. Learning more about your individual experiences can provide a starting point.

Every religious tradition has many principles, teachings, and tenets of faith. Not all people of a given tradition will understand each one. You bring into your marriage a variety of traditions and rituals that, if discussed, may enrich your own faith. Because of who you are and what your experiences have been, certain elements of your religion will hold more meaning or be more infused with emotional energy.

The Church teaches that the Church is made up of a "family of families" and the family itself gives witness to their faith and joy in God as a "domestic Church."[3] Make your home a sacred place where the two of you can worship God

3. *The Joy of Love* (*Amoris laetitia*), 87, 200. This document is an apostolic exhortation by Pope Francis.

together. Create your own rituals, prayers, and traditions that foster you as a couple. Stress the beliefs you have in common. Sharing your perceptions of God, or struggling to understand your partner's faith, and especially learning about a different religious tradition must be accomplished through respect, openness, and acceptance.

Understanding the Terminology

When you are preparing to be married, some unfamiliar terms or categorizations may be used to help determine what form of the liturgy to celebrate when you marry and how best to gear the formation to your own needs. Here are some helpful definitions to understand the nuances.

Ecumenical Marriage: Also called a *mixed marriage.* A marriage between a baptized Catholic and a baptized Christian of a non-Catholic ecclesial community. The Catholic Church recognizes the validity of baptisms celebrated in many non-Catholic ecclesial communities—for example, those of Lutherans, Presbyterians, Methodists, Baptists, and many others—any baptism that is celebrated with the right intention, using water and the Trinitarian formula (in the name of the Father, the Son, and the Holy Spirit). Because both people are baptized, an ecumenical, or mixed, marriage is sacramental.

Interfaith Marriage: The three main religious traditions—Christianity, Judaism, and Islam (Muslim)—consider themselves to be of the Abrahamic faith. Abraham was the chosen father of God's chosen people. The chosen people developed the three main religious traditions. An interfaith marriage is between a baptized Catholic and a person of the Jewish or Muslim traditions. Jewish and Muslim people are of course, not baptized. Because one person is not baptized, this marriage is valid but not sacramental. If the non-Christian should decide at a later time to be validly baptized, the marriage becomes sacramental.

Interreligious Marriage: This marriage is the union of a baptized Catholic and a person of a faith other than those of the Abrahamic faith (see above). This includes Hinduism or Buddhism. These people are of course, not baptized. Because one person is not baptized, this marriage is valid but not sacramental. Agnostics or Atheists would fall into this category. If the non-Christian should decide at a later time to be validly baptized, the marriage becomes sacramental.

Catechumen: In some cases, a baptized Catholic will marry a person who is not baptized but is seeking baptism within the Catholic Church. This person seeking Baptism is called a catechumen. A marriage between a baptized Catholic and a catechumen is valid but not sacramental, but at the time of the person's baptism, the marriage is raised to sacramental status.

Agnostic: One who does not necessarily believe in God but acknowledges the potential for him to exist.

Atheist: A person who does not believe in God.

Couple's Conversation

1. Share your experiences of God, not just your experiences of Catholicism. If we truly believe that God pursues us and is part of our lives, common ground can be built by sharing our awareness of the presence of God in our lives. One way to do this is to recall the last time you felt God present to you. Tell each other what the sights, sounds, smells, and emotions were like. Look for common elements in your perceptions as you exchange your stories of God.
2. If your future spouse does not believe in God or is agnostic, have him or her share his experiences of faith or religion. Does he or she have any experiences of something other?
3. What of your future spouses' faith do you struggle to accept or understand?
4. What type of rituals, prayers, and traditions do you think you can celebrate together?
5. If your future spouse does not believe in God or is agnostic, is he or she open to celebrating rituals together? Praying together? Do you think the lack of faith will pose long-term problems to your relationship?
6. Share with your spouse some core beliefs of your tradition, and include discussion on the symbols, rituals, and beliefs that are most important to you.
7. What has most enriched your faith by being engaged to a person of another denomination or religion?
8. Do your families support you marrying someone outside the Catholic Church? If they don't, how can you avoid this being a problem in your relationship?
9. As a couple, will you be involved in both faith communities?
10. How one expresses their faith in God composes their core identity. Faith must be honest and true to the person. One can't have two faiths. For example, you either believe in Jesus or you don't; therefore, you can't truthfully participate in the two contradictory traditions. Do you think it's important to raise your children in one faith tradition?
11. Do you agree with the Church that the Catholic person must promise to do all in his or her power to raise future children in the Catholic faith? If you are not Catholic, will you support your spouse by raising the child Catholic?
12. If you are not Catholic, is it challenging for you to go to Mass with your fiancé and not receive Communion? How do you handle these challenges?
13. Have you developed common spiritual practices? How have these practices enriched your relationship?
14. Have you decided if your wedding ceremony will take place in the Catholic Church or elsewhere?
15. How will you observe Sunday faith obligations?

Continues on next page ▶

16. How will you celebrate faith-specific holidays (Christmas, Easter, Ramadan, Passover, etc.)
17. Will the children attend a faith-based school?
18. How will you educate one another's families on your own faith tradition?
19. If you are not Catholic, what does it mean to you to know that even though you are not Catholic, the Catholic Church is praying for you and supports you in your marital journey?
20. If you are Catholic, what does it mean for you to know that the Church is praying for you and supporting you and your spouse even if he or she is not Catholic?

Healing after Abortion

If your future spouse has had an abortion (or has participated in an abortion), she will need to know that you support her and will always be present to her in a kind, loving, and accepting way. As one of God's children, you will be able to communicate his merciful love to your beloved. Most likely, she is dealing with the pain and guilt of having had an abortion, and she might be reticent to have another child. In some cases, there might be health issues related to the abortion that prevent future children. You might have even had a relationship in the past in which your own involvement contributed to an abortion. Women and men are not immune from the grief and trauma associated by abortion.

> **Forgiveness** is the most visible sign of the Father's love, which Jesus sought to reveal by his entire life.[25]
>
> —Pope Francis

First and foremost, realize that God's love is limitless and is available to those who truly and earnestly seek His forgiveness. Seek out Reconciliation. In 2016, Pope Francis gave all Catholic priests the ability to grant forgiveness for abortion. Prior to this, only a bishop or a specially appointed confessor could absolve one who had had an abortion.

More difficult is the necessity for you to forgive yourself. Forgiving yourself is part of the healing process, and God does not want you to suffer a lifetime. You can be forgiven through the sacrament of reconciliation. Pray, too, for all those who may have been involved in the abortion and those who might be considering having an abortion.

> **Comfort, give comfort my people.**
>
> —Isaiah 40:1

Your child is in the care of God. He or she desires your own joy and happiness. Know that they are loved, happy, and well cared for by God, the Father of us all. In the love of Jesus, they do not resent or condemn you. By prolonging your grief, you miss the glory which is now theirs surrounded by all the happiness in heaven.[5]

Couple's Conversation

If you have had an abortion, it is important that you are open and honest about this with your future spouse. Talk about your experiences with one another.

4. *Mercy with Misery*, 2. This is an apostolic letter by Pope Francis.
5. There is hope and help after abortion. Refer to this website for resources to help you deal with the trauma, pain, and guilt associated with abortion: hopeafterabortion.com.

Adult Children of Divorce, Abuse, Alcoholism, or Drugs

No two relationships or marriages are the same. We enter this covenant often with "issues" that may have a dark side carefully masked. These wounds can reach back to our childhood or to events that are much more recent. And if these issues are left unaddressed, they can have damaging effects on your marriage. These issues can originate from those who grew up in an abusive environment, a broken home, or with parents who were addicts.

Abuse, in any form, leaves deep and profound scars on one's emotional psyche. Studies indicate that "children who grow up in violent homes are more likely to develop alcohol and drug addictions and to become abusers themselves."[6] Can you triumph over the long-term effects of these past traumas and avoid subjecting your children to the same experience? Agreeing to live in a "barrier free" environment with your future spouse is the first step to ending the potential for this to happen.

These are not your wounds to heal alone. God is present in your union. You might falsely view your emotional baggage as yours alone, and you might fear that your future spouse will leave. No one is immune from the past-experiences of abuse or other forms of trauma and dysfunction. Trust and be open with your spouse about what you experienced, and discuss together how these issues might affect your marriage.

Ask yourself these questions, answering from what you observe about your future spouse. (Refer to the domestic abuse questions on page 65).

- Have you noticed if your future spouse abuses alcohol or drugs?
- Does he or she try to hide alcohol use form you?
- Are there co-dependency issues?
- Does your significant other lie? Do they try to cover up things? Are they secretive?
- Do you try to cover up actions for your significant other?
- Do you argue about alcohol and drugs?

Couple's Conversation

Allow your future spouse the opportunity to talk about their situation. Be patient, kind, and compassionate toward his or her pain. Be present to them as you listen to how their experiences have shaped their lives. Consider how it still affects them today and how this might affect your union.

Domestic Violence Awareness

When a couple exchanges consent to marry, they vow (or promise) to honor one another. With the exchange of consent, you are making a promise that your marriage will always be loving and respectful. This vow to honor and respect applies to both husbands and wives, calling you into a partnership of equal dignity. Men and women are both created in the image of God. While many spouses understand this call to mutuality and equal authority in marriage, others enter marriage with destructive attitudes about how men and women should relate to one another. According to the bishops of the United States, "Marriage must never be a struggle for control."[7]

The Center for Disease Control and Prevention reports that "About 1 in 4 women and nearly 1 in 10 men have experienced sexual violence, physical violence, and/or stalking by an intimate partner during their lifetime and reported some form of intimate partner

---

6. *When I Cry for Help: A Pastoral Response to Domestic Violence Against Women*, a document from the United States Conference of Catholic Bishops.
7. *Follow the Way of Love*, a pastoral message of the United States Catholic Bishops to families, paragraph 19.

violence-related impact."[8] Simply raising the issue during marriage preparation may help an individual or a couple seek assistance. Because it happens in Catholic marriages, we want you to have information you can use for yourself or share with family and friends.

Domestic violence, also called intimate partner violence, usually creeps into a relationship slowly. Any couple will experience occasional arguments, but healthy conflict resolution will involve both parties working respectfully on a solution that is fair to both of them. Abusive relationships, on the other hand, have a well-established pattern of behavior marked by rigid control and manipulation. Use of pornography, drugs, or alcohol are often related to domestic abuse. Often, survivors do not recognize abusive behavior developing until much later when it becomes glaringly obvious. For that reason, it is important for people to know how to recognize abuse in its early stages and for victims to seek advice from a professional domestic violence counselor.

Domestic violence is defined as a pattern of behavior that seeks power and control over an intimate partner. This negative power and control may be shown in physical, verbal, sexual, or economic ways. Verbal or emotional abuse is the most common form, but it is not always recognized as abuse. When partners see their relationship developing hurtful behaviors, they need to examine what is happening. Sometimes domestic abuse begins with small measures of control and slowly escalates. The first signs of control may even seem reasonable, for example when a spouse insists: "Don't spend time with family and friends, I want you to spend all your free time with me." This may seem reasonable until one realizes it is the first step in isolating someone from family and friends.

Treating each other daily with love and dignity is critical for a good marriage. However, the Church realizes that loving behavior is not always practiced, and she offers two foundational pieces of information to guide couples.

The Church addresses domestic abuse in her laws about the sacrament of marriage: "If either spouse causes grave mental or physical danger to the other spouse or to the offspring or otherwise renders common life too difficult, that spouse gives the other a legitimate cause for leaving, either by decree of the local ordinary or even on his or her own authority if there is danger in delay."[9]

The United States Catholic Bishops have written an informative and compassionate pastoral statement, *When I Call for Help: A Pastoral Response to Violence Against Women*, in which they state: "When violence occurs within a sacramental marriage, the abused spouse may question, 'How do these violent acts relate to my promise to take my spouse for better or for worse?' The person being assaulted needs to know that acting to end the abuse does not violate the marriage promises. While violence can be directed towards men, it tends to harm women and children more."[10]

Verbal requests for forgiveness unaccompanied by changed behavior are inadequate. Victims of domestic violence should not be urged or pressured to forgive. Most victims want to forgive, but forgiving is a process that requires time. Sometimes the wounds are so deep or the threat so real that reconciliation is not possible or advisable. Safety is the first concern, and adequate time to heal is necessary.

There Is Help

When someone wonders if their own or their partner's behavior is abusive, they should seek individual counseling with someone trained in domestic violence. Domestic violence counseling is generally provided free of charge at domestic violence service agencies and should be sought

8. Centers for Disease Control and Prevention, "Preventing Intimate Partner Violence," www.cdc.gov/violenceprevention/intimatepartnerviolence/fastfact.html.

9. *Code of Canon Law*, 1153 §1.

10. This document is available on the website of the United States Conference of Catholic Bishops: www.usccb.org/issues-and-action/marriage-and-family/marriage/domestic-violence/when-i-call-for-help.cfm.

even when the person is unsure about what is happening.

The National Domestic Violence Hotline provides crisis intervention or advice, and referrals to local service providers. Call 800-799-SAFE (7233) or 800-787-3224 (TTY). Email assistance is available at ndvh@ndvh.org. Help is available for both those who are experiencing abuse and for those who abuse. In *When I Call for Help*, the United States Catholic Bishops urge friends and pastoral ministers to attend first to the safety of victims and their children. When a relationship ends, friends and Church ministers can aid victims and family in mourning the loss and supporting the survivors.

Further information about how Catholics can respond to domestic violence is available from organizations like the Archdiocese of Chicago's Domestic Violence Outreach (www.domesticviolenceoutreach.org) and Catholics for Family Peace Education and Research Initiative (www.catholicsforfamilypeace.org).

For Private Reflection

These questions are for individuals to consider privately. The responses will not be discussed in the group nor will they be collected or shared with others. Spend some time individually examining your relationship with your future spouse. This engagement period is the perfect time to ensure that you are both committed to a safe and healthy relationship. The questions below are related to early warning signs of domestic violence. Abusive behaviors generally escalate over time. If you see these behaviors in your current relationship, seek individual counseling from a domestic violence counselor now. Do not wait until after the wedding to seek counsel. While we cannot change other people, we can decide how we will be treated

1. Does your partner continually make you account for your time, where you are going, how you spend money, or who you are visiting?
2. Is your partner often jealous or accuse you of being unfaithful?
3. Is your partner ever rude to your friends or family?
4. Is your partner overly critical of your appearance, your cooking, your ideas, etc.?
5. Does your partner often reject or dismiss your ideas?
6. Does your partner become angry more easily if he or she is drinking?
7. Do you quarrel much over financial matters or over having children?
8. Does your partner pressure you for sex or sexual acts you don't like?
9. Has your partner thrown or broken things when angry?
10. Has your partner ever struck you or threatened to harm you or your children or your pets?

Answering yes to any of these questions is a cause of concern, and you should seek individual domestic violence counseling about your relationship. Do not overlook or minimize suspected abuse in your relationship. Although these issues may be difficult to discuss, the tragic fact is that domestic violence is a common reality. If domestic abuse is suspected, do not go to a marriage counselor who is not trained in domestic violence. Do not think you will be able to fix this problem by simply talking with your partner. If after appropriate counseling you learn the problem is not domestic violence, then by all means work on your relationship.

Dealing with the Stress of Wedding Preparations

As your wedding date gets closer, you two will get busier and busier with all the details of preparing your big day. There will be many things demanding your attention, and many decisions will need to be made by the two of you.

> It is good that your wedding be simple and make what is truly important stand out. Some are more concerned with the exterior details; with the banquet, the photographs, the clothes, the flowers . . . These are important for a celebration, but only if they point to the real reason for your joy: the Lord's blessing on your love.
>
> —Pope Francis

Your wedding day is important. But even more important are the years of marriage that follow, the day-to-day decisions to love each other "for better or for worse." Five years from now—maybe even just one or two years from now, you won't remember all the little details that didn't go quite right, the glitches that most of your guests won't even know about at all.

If you can develop good habits now of praying together and respecting each other's opinions and feelings, those good habits have the potential to last many years and to enrich and strengthen your relationship. There will be some things on your wedding day that are totally out of your control, but the less you fret about them the more joyful your day will be.

What is important on your wedding day is that you celebrate a sacred occasion, the sacrament of your marriage among loving family and friends, supported by their prayer and blessing and that of the Church. You are looking forward to a long life together, and the blessing of children borne out of your love for one another. What is important now is that you maintain your loving relationship with each other and with God. The dress will be put away, the flowers will fade, but your love for each other and your faith in God will endure and will carry you through many years of a happy and fruitful marriage. That's really what this is all about, isn't it?

Appendix 2
Building a Healthy Marriage

Enriching Your Marriage

The wedding liturgy is clear that you are "no longer . . . two, but one flesh." The dream of a shared life and the blessing of becoming "one flesh" is both joyful and challenging. The way you interact and share your life glorifies God as one body. To glorify "the Lord by your life" is a daunting and challenging task. Setting goals for your marriage can help you in the tasks of being open and honest with one another and establishing realistic expectations for your marriage.

Because your marriage is a reflection of God's love, be assured of his presence in your marriage. He is right there with you, helping you, guiding you, and loving you. But you must also work toward your goal of becoming "one flesh." Be intentional about planning and setting goals.

Enriching your marriage is encouraged. This means you must find and make time to be with each other, to make each other a priority (even after children!), and to talk about your thoughts, feelings, and hopes for the future. It means joining hearts and minds in order to set goals together—not just once, but routinely adjusting goals to meet the realities of work, family, health, and other factors.

It is also important to acknowledge that your spouse will never fully complete you. And it isn't his or her responsibility to do so! Only God can fulfill a human being. Humans are flawed and imperfect, and expecting your spouse to complete you is an unfair burden to place upon him or her.

There is no perfect life, no perfect job, no perfect childhood, no perfect marriage, and no perfect set of people who will always do what we expect them to do. What we have is a perfect God who is able to lead us through this imperfect life with unfailing strength, incomparable wisdom, and infinite love.[1]

1. Author unknown; posted on the *Mindful Christianity* Facebook page, accessed December 29, 2019.

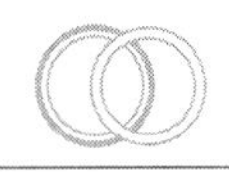

Twenty-Five Tips from Pope Francis

Here is some helpful advice for keeping your marriage strong. This list was compiled from the wisdom of Pope Francis as offered in his document *The Joy of Love* as well as the various audiences he has had with newly engaged and married couples.[2]

1. Love takes work. Be patient.
2. Offer yourself to the other as gift.
3. Share each other's joys, hopes, dreams, challenges, griefs, anxieties, and day-to-day occurrences.
4. Make time for one another.
5. Keep the romance alive.
6. Say please, thank you, and I'm sorry.
7. Trust is important; honor your commitments, and be true to your promises.
8. Show your love with actions, not just words.
9. Be gentle and thoughtful; not rude or impolite.
10. Listen.
11. When you argue, acknowledge your partner's perspective.
12. Disagreements are ok; but have them without hurting your partner.
13. Help your spouse reach his or her greatest potential.
14. Rejoice with your spouse's accomplishments, and don't boast over your own.
15. Believe in your partner; don't be angry, jealous, or resentful.
16. Accept your spouse's shortcomings, and understand and acknowledge their imperfections and quirks.
17. Develop your own gifts and talents; it's important to be an interesting person.
18. Never go to bed angry; hugs help!
19. Don't hold grudges or pass blame.
20. Don't lose hope even when times are difficult.
21. Ask for permission (be courteous and communicate about plans).
22. Try to find your partner beautiful and loveable, even when this might be difficult.
23. Have a sense of humor.
24. Try to have good sex.
25. Don't give up on each other; have faith in each other and in God.

---

2. Pope Francis' *The Joy of Love* (or by its Latin title, *Amoris laetita*) is available on the Vatican website (www.vatican.va). It is an extremely pastoral exhortation that acknowledges the day-to-day struggles that couples face, with guidance for strengthening their commitment to one another.

Opening Prayer

The facilitator will welcome those present and invite you to take a moment of silence and become aware that you are in the presence of God. He or she will then invite you to stand.

Facilitator: O God, come to my assistance.

All make the Sign of the Cross on himself or herself.

All: Lord, make haste to help me.

Facilitator: Glory to the Father, and to the Son, and to the Holy Spirit,

All bow while saying the beginning of this prayer.

All: as it was in the beginning, is now, and will be forever.

All: Amen.

Hymn *Lord of All Hopefulness*

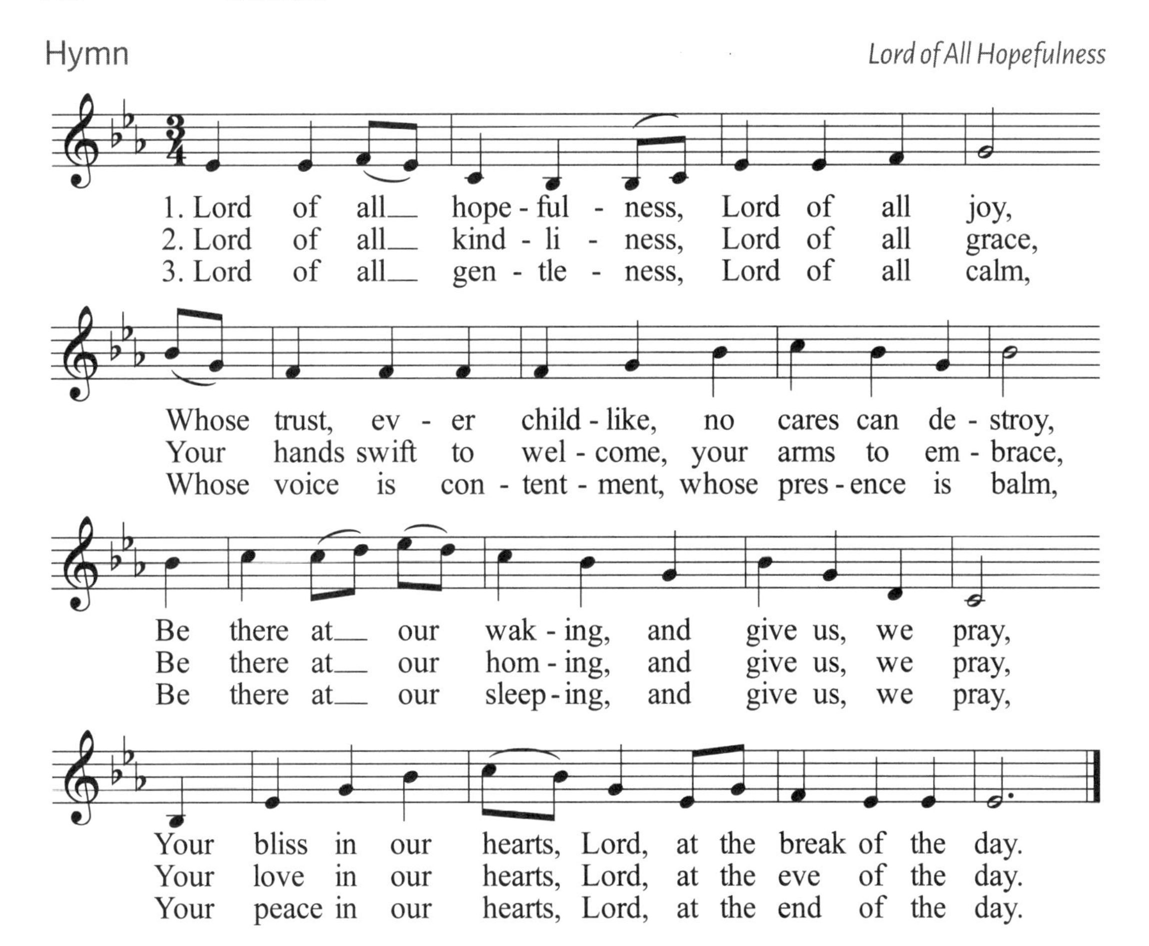

Jan Struther, 1901-1953, © Oxford University Press; Tune: SLANE, 10 11 11 12.

All are seated for the Word of God.

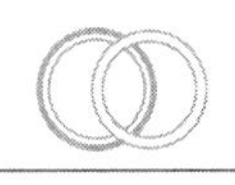

Psalm 103

1–2, 8 and 13, 17–18a

All recite the antiphon and the verses of the psalm together. This psalm is one of the options for your wedding liturgy.

Facilitator: The Lord is kind and merciful.

All: **The Lord is kind and merciful.**
Bless the LORD, O my soul,
and all within me, his holy name.
Bless the LORD, O my soul,
and never forget all his benefits.

The LORD is compassionate and gracious,
slow to anger and rich in mercy.
As a father has compassion on his children,

the LORD's compassion is on those who fear him.
But the mercy of the LORD is everlasting
upon those who hold him in fear,
upon children's children his righteousness,
for those who keep his covenant.

Facilitator: The Lord is kind and merciful.

All: **The Lord is kind and merciful.**

Scripture Reading

1 Corinthians 13:4–13

This reading is one of the options for your wedding liturgy.

Reader: The Word of the Lord.

All: **Thanks be to God.**

Reflection

The Joy of Love (Amoris laetita), 98, 99, 100, and 119 by Pope Francis

Moment of Silence

Intercessions

All stand for for the intercessions.

All: **Lord of Love, hear our prayer.**

Our Father

Closing Prayer

Dismissal

All make the Sign of the Cross on themselves while the facilitator offers the closing prayer.
All respond, "Amen."

Facilitator: May we have a fruitful reflection and a beautiful day.

All: **Thanks be to God.**

Closing Prayer

All stand for the opening song. Sing verses one and two.

Opening Song

Love Divine, All Loves Excelling

Charles Wesley, 1707-1788, alt.; Tune: HYFRYDOL, 8 7 8 7 D; Rowland H. Prichard, 1811-1887.

Facilitator: In the name of the Father, and of the Son, and of the Holy Spirit.

All: **Amen.**

Facilitator: Brothers and sisters,
let us praise our Lord Jesus Christ,
who loved us and gave himself up for us.

All: **Amen.**

If the facilitator is a priest or deacon, the following greeting and response is used.

Priest/Deacon: Grace to you and peace
from our Lord Jesus Christ,
who loved us and gave himself up for us.

All: **And with your spirit.**

Opening Remarks / Prayer

The assembly responds "Amen" to the opening prayer and all are seated for the Word of God.

Psalm 128

1–2, 3, 4–5ac and 6a

All recite the antiphon and the verses of the psalm together. This psalm is one of the options for your wedding liturgy.

Facilitator: Blessed are those who fear the Lord.

All: **Blessed are those who fear the Lord.**

Blessed are all who fear the LORD,
and walk in his ways!
By the labor of your hands you shall eat.
You will be blessed and prosper.

Your wife like a fruitful vine
in the heart of your house;
your children like shoots of the olive
around your table.

Indeed thus shall be blessed
the man who fears the LORD.
May the LORD bless you from Zion
all the days of your life!
May you see your children's children.

Facilitator: Blessed are those who fear the Lord.

All: **Blessed are those who fear the Lord.**

Scripture Reading

Romans 15:1b–3a, 5–7, 13

This reading is one of the options for your wedding liturgy.

Reader: The Word of the Lord.

All: Thanks be to God.

Reflection

Dogmatic Constitution on the Church, 11

Intercessions

All stand for the intercessions.

All: Keep us in your love forever, Lord.

Prayer of Blessing

Facilitator: We give you praise, O Lord,
who in your gentle wisdom call and prepare
your son and daughter to love each other.
Graciously strengthen their hearts, we pray,
so that, by keeping faith and pleasing you in all things,
they may come happily to the Sacrament of Marriage.
Through Christ our Lord.

All: Amen.

Closing Remarks

Dismissal

Facilitator: May the God of love and peace
dwell within you,
direct your steps,
and strengthen your hearts in his love.

All: Amen.

Closing Song

Love Divine, All Loves Excelling

Sing verse three of the closing song. *It is found on page 72.*

Facilitator: Go in peace, loving and serving the Lord.

All: Thanks be to God.

Marriage and Family Resources

Marriage Resources from LTP

The following resources are published by Liturgy Training Publications, an agency of the Archdiocese of Chicago (www.LTP.org). They will help you and your future spouse prepare your wedding liturgy, reflect on the meaning of marriage, develop a prayer life, and strengthen your commitment to one another throughout your life.

The Meaning of Marriage

Living the Mystery of Marriage: Building Your Sacramental Life Together: In this work, the author, Perry J. Cahall, introduces engaged and recently married couples to living the vocation of marriage in its spiritual and moral dimensions.

A Marriage Sourcebook: A collection of scripture passages, reflections from theologians, and excerpts from poems, hymns, and prayers related to marriage. It is organized by the theological aspects of marriage.

A New Vision of Family Life: A Reflection on Amoris laetitia: In 2016, Pope Francis issued his apostolic exhortation on love and marriage, *The Joy of Love* (or, as known in Latin, *Amoris laetitia*). In this book, Rev. Louis J. Cameli travels with couples while unpacking this document. It will help support families through difficult times, aid them in discerning their conscience, and help integrate them into the life of the parish community. This book situates marriage and family life as a central focus for transformation in the Christian life.

Preparing the Wedding Liturgy

A Guide to Catholic Weddings: Q&A for Couples: This resource, written by Sandra Dooley, provides answers to common questions engaged couples have about the Catholic Church and the wedding ceremony. It is perfect to use together and will help answer questions related to wedding ceremony preparations and Church regulations.

United in Christ: Preparing the Liturgy of the Word at Catholic Weddings: Designed as a formational tool, *United in Christ* guides couples through each of the possible readings from the wedding liturgy, providing brief scripture commentary from Catholic scholars and liturgical ministers that explain the meaning of the scripture text through the lens of the needs of the couple. Along with the full text of each reading, this resource also offers insight into why a couple may choose a particular reading. It is also available in Spanish.

Prayer Resources

At Home with the Word: This resource will guide you to a deeper understanding of the Sunday scriptures, providing the readings for this liturgical year, insights from scripture scholars, and action steps. It will help root your faith in the scriptures and provide practical ways for you to act upon this faith. It is updated each year. A Spanish version, *Palabra de Dios*, is also available and newly updated each year.

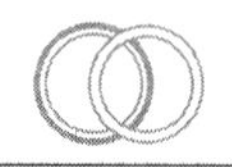

Catholic Household Blessings and Prayers: This book contains all the essential Catholic prayers as well as blessings and prayers for the most important moments in life. It will help couples and families develop rituals within the home. Although published by the United States Conference of Catholic Bishops, it is also available through Liturgy Training Publications.

Catholic Prayers, Second Edition: This pocket-sized book includes familiar Catholic prayers.

Celebrating Sunday for Catholic Families: This simple booklet provides parents with material to use at home with their school-age children in order to pray, break open the Sundayscriptures, and enrich their experience attending Mass as a family. For every Sunday and holyday of obligation of the school year, plus summer, the booklet includes a brief passage from scripture, a short reflection, two conversation questions (one to do in the car on the way to Mass and one to do in the car on the way home), and a suggested activity. The ultimate goal of this resource is to provide a very simple and approachable way for families to integrate prayer, scripture, and Sunday Mass attendance into their lives. It is updated each year. A Spanish edition is also available.

Daily Prayer: Easy-to-use for group and individual prayer, *Daily Prayer* centers on a scripture reading each day, along with a reflection, a psalm, intercessions, and closing prayer. It draws on the long tradition of *lectio divina*, providing a simple order of prayer for each day of the liturgical year and will help individuals, couples, and families pray at set times of day. A new edition is available each year.

Prayerbook for Engaged Couples, Fourth Edition: This practical book helps couples discuss, pray over, and choose the scriptures that will be proclaimed at their wedding. It also invites them to pray with the words of the marriage rite and the Mass and offers a brief reflection and questions for discussion on each. It also includes additional prayers and blessings pertinent to the lives of engaged couples. Use of this book will allow couples to develop a practice of prayer and reflection that will sustain them throughout their married life. Although primarily used for the period of engagement, revisiting these prayers, especially the vows, will help strengthen your married life. A Spanish edition is available.

Reconciliation Resources

The Sacrament of Reconciliation: *Encountering the Mercy of God in Your Marriage:* Couples participating in marriage formation are encouraged to participate in the sacrament of reconciliation before they marry and to continue to take part in this sacrament throughout their marriage. Written by Timothy P. O'Malley and Danielle Noe, this free PDF provides a reflection on reconciliation and offers an Examination of Conscience for married couples. It is also available in Spanish. The English product is available here: www.ltp.org/products/details/ESR/sacrament-of-reconciliation.

Discipleship

Baptized for Discipleship: The Meaning of Baptism for Our Christian Life: Written by Mary A. Ehle, this short resource provides a reflection on the sacrament of baptism and how it changes us to live as Christian disciples in the world.

From Mass to Mission: Understanding the Mass and Its Significance for Our Christian Life: Paul Turner and Trish Sullivan Vanni explore the meaning of the Mass and how it forms us to be Christ's light in the world.

Marriage Enrichment Websites

The following websites provide material for those preparing for marriage and enrichment for married couples and for those in troubled marriages:

- The Archdiocese of Chicago provides resources and reflections on marriage preparation: pvm.archchicago.org/lifelong-formation/marriage-and-family-ministries/
- For Your Marriage: www.foryourmarriage.org
- The Retrouvaille Program: www.helpourmarriage.org
- Catholic Therapists: www.catholictherapists.com/
- Marriage Therapists: www.marriagefriendlytherapists.com/
- Chicago Counseling: www.catholiccharities.net/GetHelp/OurServices/Counseling/Holbrook.aspx
- Family Bridges: familybridgesusa.com/
- Worldwide Marriage Encounter: www.wwme.org/
- FOCCUS, Inc. USA: www.foccusinc.com/

Couples may continue their education on Natural Family Planning and receive more information on the following websites.

- Billings Ovulation Method: learnNFPonline.com
- Creighton Method: www.creightonmodel.com/
- Sympto-Thermal Method: ccli.org/learn
- Sympto-Thermal Method: www.symtopro.org
- Marquette Method: www.mmnfp.com/